Holy Envy

ALSO BY BARBARA BROWN TAYLOR

Leaving Church
An Altar in the World
Learning to Walk in the Dark

Holy Envy

FINDING GOD *in the* FAITH *of* OTHERS

Barbara Brown Taylor

HarperOne
An Imprint of HarperCollins*Publishers*

HarperOne

FIRST HARPERCOLLINS PAPERBACK EDITION PUBLISHED IN 2020

Designed by Michelle Crowe

Chapter opener art from cover image and by barka, basel101658, elisabetaaa, Potapov Alexander, RetroClipArt /Shutterstock, Inc.

Library of Congress Cataloging-in-Publication Data is available upon request.

ISBN 978-0-06-240657-6

23 24 25 26 27 LBC 11 10 9 8 7

For
Ray Cleere, who hired me,
James Mellichamp, who retired me,
and Timothy Lytle, my closest ally all along

And silently their shining Lord replies:
"I am a mirror set before your eyes,
And all who come before my splendor see
Themselves, their own unique reality;
You came as thirty birds and therefore saw
These selfsame thirty birds, not less nor more;
If you had come as forty, fifty—here
An answering forty, fifty would appear;
Though you have struggled, wandered, traveled far,
It is yourselves you see and what you are."

FROM *The Conference of the Birds* BY
FARĪD UD-DĪN 'AṬṬĀR, TRANSLATED BY
DICK DAVIS AND AFKHAM DARBANDI

A Note on Creative Nonfiction

I have taught world religions at the college level for almost twenty years now. When I began, I did not know that I would be writing a book about it in the future. Although many of my memories remain clear to me, I cannot back them up with transcripts or recordings. Where I have told the stories of others, I have disguised their identities or left them easy to identify, depending on what they asked me to do when they gave me their permission. In some cases I have gathered memories from several different years and put them into the same time frame. In every case I have told the truth to the best of my ability, fully aware of how many tricks memory can play. The best disclaimer I have ever heard is broadcast at the beginning of every *Moth Radio Hour*, my favorite program on public radio: "Moth stories are true as remembered and affirmed by the storyteller." So are mine.

Barbara Brown Taylor
Clarkesville, Georgia
April 1, 2018

Contents

Introduction: The Smaller Picture   I

1:    Religion 101   13

2:    Vishnu's Almonds   27

3:    Wave Not Ocean   45

4:    Holy Envy   61

5:    The Nearest Neighbors   81

6:    Disowning God   101

7:    The Shadow-Bearers   121

8:    Failing Christianity   139

9:    Born Again   161

10:    Divine Diversity   175

11:    The God You Didn't Make Up   187

12:    The Final Exam   203

Epilogue: Church of the Common Ground   215

Acknowledgments   225

Notes   229

Recommended Reading   235

Holy Envy

Introduction:
The Smaller Picture

What do they know of England, who only England know?

RUDYARD KIPLING

The book in your hands is a small window on a large subject. Set at a private liberal arts college in the foothills of the Appalachians, it is the story of a Christian minister who lost her way in the church and found a new home in the classroom, where the course she taught most often was not Introduction to the New Testament, Church History, or Christian Theology, but Religions of the World. As soon as she recovered from the shock of meeting God in so many new hats, she fell for every religion she taught. When she taught Judaism, she wanted to be a rabbi. When she taught Buddhism, she wanted to be a monk. It was only when she taught Christianity that the fire sputtered, because her religion looked so different once she saw it lined up with the others. She always promised her students that studying other faiths would not make them lose their own. Then she lost hers, or at least the one she started out with. This is the story of how that happened and what happened next.

It is my story, but it is also the story of a generation of young Americans who are growing up with more religious diversity than their parents or grandparents did and who are still trying to decide whether this is a good thing or a bad thing. The Christians among them can sense the anxiety in their churches, where changing the music and hiring more millennial pastors have not brought the young people back. Will the Christianity they know best survive, or is it dying of old age? Is the Holy Spirit at work in what is going on, or is a more sinister spirit at work?

Some are questioning whether the churches they grew up in have anything to offer them as they make their ways in a culture of many cultures with many views of truth, some of which make a great deal of sense to them. For those who counted on God to protect them from so many choices, it is as if the heavenly Father let go of their hand in a crowd one day and vanished into a sea of divine possibilities. I cannot protect the students in my classes from this any better than I can protect myself. Existential dizziness is one of the side effects of higher education, and it affects teachers too.

I came to the classroom through the back door. Parish ministry was my front-door job, the one I had been doing for fifteen years when the president of a nearby college called and said there was an opening for someone to teach religion. Would I be interested? I said no the first time. My only credentials were a master's degree in divinity, deep immersion in one Christian denomination, and a lifelong curiosity about religion. All three were do-it-myself projects, since my parents had worked hard to protect me from God while I was growing up. When I was fifteen, I found my father sitting cross-legged in the dining room meditating in front of a biofeedback machine. When I told my mother I wanted to be baptized, she told me I would get over it. Both had such a poor opinion of religion that they raised my two younger sisters and me to believe in higher education instead of a higher power. We went to the library every week, not church. We read Shakespeare, not the Bible.

This left me little choice but to rebel by joining every church in driving distance as soon as I got my license. I was Baptist for a while, then Presbyterian. In college I was an evangelical Christian who hung out with Methodist seminarians during the week and ate supper with Catholics on Sunday nights. But casual conversations were not enough. I wanted thick books, smart teachers, hard theological nuts to crack. I became a religion major, finding more of what I was looking for in the classroom than I had ever found in church. When my adviser suggested seminary, I went, with no ambition but to learn as much as I could about the divine mysteries of the universe from anyone willing to teach me more. A divinity school sounded like exactly the right place.

My favorite professor was an Episcopal priest who taught New Testament with nothing but a tiny Greek edition open on the table in front of him. Above the table he was immaculate, dressed in a black clergy shirt with a starched linen collar and a worsted wool jacket that made him look like a duke. Under the table he wore laced-up leather hunting boots with mud on them, as if he had barely made it to class on time after an early morning walk in the woods. He showed up in my dreams. He also taught me a great deal about the New Testament. When he returned my essays, every page was marked with neatly circled numbers that matched his handwritten comments on lined pages at the back.

No one had ever paid such careful attention to my scholarship, so when I sought him out for spiritual guidance, I did exactly what he said: I began attending Mass at the Anglo-Catholic church downtown, where the divine mysteries on display exceeded anything in my prior experience. Though I quickly learned how to genuflect, chant psalms, and cross myself at the name of the Trinity, it took me a full year to work up the nerve to take Communion. I was too afraid I would do something that caused the Communion wafer to combust in my palm— reach out with the wrong hand, for instance, or fail to confess a particularly subtle sin. When I finally found the courage to approach the altar rail and nothing terrible happened, I became a confirmed Episcopalian. The combination of fixed prayer and free thought was exactly what I had been looking for. It was the last church I joined, and the one I still call home.

Ordination was out of the question at the time, since the Episcopal church did not admit women to the priesthood until after my graduation from divinity school. Several years later, when things changed, I completed all the requirements for receiving what are still called "holy orders." The bishop signed the papers, the date was set, and in due time I knelt before the altar of a beautiful church with gold crosses painted on the red ceiling, holding very still as my soon-to-be-fellow priests gathered around to lay their hands on my head.

In the years that followed I got as close to the divine mysteries as I could. I learned to perform baptisms, marriages, house blessings, and funerals. I learned how to name and handle all the ritual items involved in a Sunday celebration of Holy Communion: chalice, paten, flagon, ciborium, pall, corporal, purificator, lavabo. I learned which vestments to wear on which occasions and how to hold my hands when I pronounced the benediction at the end of every service. As an alchemist of God's grace, I was allowed into the most private rooms of people's lives, which gave me a more spacious heart. In exchange for these privileges I attended dozens of committee meetings, ordered reams of Sunday school materials, proofread hundreds of church newsletters, and filed drawers full of annual reports.

It was a good life for a long time. Then it was not. Ask me what happened, and I can offer you a variety of stories that are all true: I was not a skilled leader; I was gone too much; I succumbed to compassion fatigue; I lost faith in the church. All these years later there is another story that sounds as true as any of those, which goes like this: the same Spirit that called me into the church called me out again, to learn the difference between the living water and the well. As surely as priesthood had given me a sturdy bucket for dipping into that well—and as clearly as I could smell the elemental depths of the divine mystery every time I bent over to draw some of it up—the well was not the water. It was a container and not the source. My Episcopal well, beloved as it was, was no longer enough for me to live on. I was dry as a bone.

That was when the president of the nearby college called to ask if I might be interested in teaching religion. I said yes this time. It was the best way I could think of to start learning again—about buckets and wells other than my own this time, about other ways of approaching the divine mystery that were strange enough to upset my parched equilibrium. In short order I traded an altar for a desk, a pulpit for a whiteboard, a parish register for a roll book, and a black clergy shirt for a green dress.

My first class met at 8:00 a.m. in a room that could have passed for an autopsy suite. The cinder-block walls were painted slick white. A poster of the periodic table sagged from the bulletin board. The trash can needed emptying. I lined up a row of religious symbols on my desk, so there would be something to point to when students asked if they were in the right room: a brass menorah, a large image of Shiva, a seated Buddha, a carved

wooden cross, and an open copy of the Qur'an on a stand. I
plugged a boom box into the wall and put on a disc from the Fez
Music Festival in Morocco, which drowned out the buzz from
the fluorescent lights overhead.

Two dozen students drifted into the room over the next few
minutes, pausing a moment at the door and then choosing their
places at one of the long tables. One girl went straight to a chair
in the front row, opened a three-ring binder to a blank page,
and wrote "Religion 101" at the top. Two big guys in athletic
jackets headed to the back row, where they sat eating tater tots
and scrambled eggs covered with cheese out of Styrofoam boxes.
At 8:05 a.m. I welcomed everyone to class, so high on first-day
adrenaline that some of the students shrank back as I strode
among them passing out syllabi.

The stapled sheets of paper looked so official that even I believed in them. They had required and recommended books on
them. They had a bulleted list of learning outcomes. They included a summary of graded assignments, guidelines for written
work, a point system for attendance, and warnings about late
papers. There was a complete class schedule at the end, which
had worked out perfectly with the chapters in the textbook. We
would spend five class sessions on each major world religion,
with a ten-point quiz at the end of each unit, two short papers
on topics of the students' own choosing, and a final exam. Those
assignments, plus ten more points for attendance, added up to a
perfect one hundred.

Laid out like that, it looked completely doable. Students who
could not distinguish Hinduism from Buddhism would be able
to describe the differences between them by the end. Students
who knew nothing about the division between Protestants and
Catholics would be able to explain it to their roommates. In

these ways and more, they would learn enough about the great religions of the world to think more deeply about what they believed and why. By the end of the course, their religious literacy would have taken a giant leap, equipping them to be better neighbors in both their personal and professional lives.

That was my welcome speech, more or less. By the time I finished it, the girl in the front row had gone through her syllabus with a yellow highlighter and taken a full page of notes. The two guys in the back had finished their breakfasts. A ginger-headed fellow in the middle had fallen asleep with his head on his arm and was breathing wetly through his mouth. When I asked for questions, there were a few about excused absences and whether it was okay to wear hats in class. Then the students were gone, apparently confident that I knew where we were going.

If I thought I did, it was because I had never been there before. I was on the first leg of a whole new journey, starting out in a covered wagon full of carefully selected supplies, a map on the seat beside me with a clear path drawn from the first day of class to the last. At this point I do not even remember when the compass broke or how many times I had to revise the map, because it did not match the territory. What I do remember is that I got exactly what I wanted: new views of the divine mystery, new worlds of meaning, new buckets for lowering into new wells, new words to describe the living water I fetched up.

The mistake was to think I could add these to the old Christian ones that had served me so well for so long with no upsetting consequences. The problem was that I could not teach other people's religions without loving them as I loved my own, or at least giving it my best shot. This turned out to be much more difficult than I thought.

Contrary to popular opinion, all religions are *not* alike. Their

followers see the world in very distinct ways. Their understandings of the human condition proceed from different assumptions, leading them to propose different remedies. If I had been
able to resist the wisdom they offered me—if I had been able to
keep my Christian glasses on, so that I only saw what those pre-
scription lenses allowed me to see—then I might have emerged
unchanged. But that is not how it went for me.

Instead, I found things to envy in all of the traditions I taught.
Some were compatible with Christian faith, like the Jewish Sabbath or the Buddhist focus on compassion. Others forced a choice,
like the Muslim understanding that God has no offspring or the
Hindu view that humans create their own destiny through many
lifetimes. This left some important questions on the table. Is there
a sovereign God who rules the cosmos or not? Can someone else
die on a cross for my sins or not? As much as I envied the spiritual
independence of people who answered "not" to those questions,
my tradition depended on "yes" answers to both of them. Could
I still learn something by taking the opposite answers seriously?
Could my faith be improved by the faith of others?

Clearly, the answer to that last question was yes, or you would
not be holding this book in your hands. But this is not the book
I set out to write. I wanted to write a book about teaching world
religions to undergraduates at a small rural college in northeast
Georgia, with students in all the starring roles. The plan was to
narrate what they learned, how they learned it, and why it was
important for you to learn it too, at least if you want to make better sense of the dizzying new world in which you live. I wanted
to offer insights that would not cost you anything. I wanted to
make life easier for you.

Fortunately, that book refused to be written. What took its
place is a book about the teacher of the class, not the students,

and what she learned about the high cost of seeing the divine mystery through other people's eyes. As the title suggests, it is a book about how my envy of other traditions turned into holy envy, offering me the chance to be born again within my own tradition. It will take me a while to get there, but since the classroom remains my small window on a large subject, you need to know something about Piedmont College and the rural county where it was founded in 1897.

Legend has it that some of the first students arrived barefoot, with their parents pulling a live pig on a rope behind them in exchange for tuition. After the first president, a Methodist minister named Spence, cashed in his own life insurance policy to keep the place going, he turned to the American Missionary Board of the Congregational Church for help. Since 1901, Piedmont has gone forward as an independent, church-related, four-year liberal arts institution in Demorest, Georgia. Today the student body hovers around twenty-three hundred. The student–faculty ratio is fourteen to one. Some students are the first in their families to go to college.

Piedmont means "foot-mountain," which is an exaggeration, since most of the mountains are in the next county, but "foot-hill" works, since the campus is nestled in the lower swells of the Appalachians. There are still pig sheds and chicken houses nearby, along with one of the largest poultry producers in the country. According to the Chamber of Commerce, slightly more than 43,000 people lived in Habersham County in 2010, with 1,823 of them in the two-stoplight town of Demorest. This means Piedmont students outnumber full-time residents, with whom they share a very short main street with the post office and city hall on one side and a restaurant and the college art gallery on the other.

What the Chamber website does not say is that Demorest was once a "sundown town," where "colored people" were not welcome after dark. Now Habersham County is home to significant numbers of people with roots in Central America, along with smaller populations of Southeast Asian and African Americans. Though there are not enough Jews to make a quorum for prayer or enough Muslims to keep a halal butcher in business, there are enough Buddhists to support a temple nine miles south of the college, which means that it is not unusual to see a monk in orange robes testing the ripeness of the mangoes at the Super Walmart. College students hang out there too, since it is the closest thing they have to a mall. There is one movie theater in the county, one bowling alley, three rivers, and sixty-two churches.

As this suggests, most of my students identify as Christian. Though they come from twenty states and ten countries, they go to school in what the writer Flannery O'Connor once called "the Christ-haunted South," where Christianity is as mainstream as Coca-Cola and traveling evangelists still set up striped tents by the side of the road in the summertime. Christianity is in the water here. It is in the air and soil. Students who arrive from large public high schools in suburban areas are sometimes surprised by the shortage of cultural diversity on campus, both in the student body and among the faculty. At the same time, they value their small classes and the close friendships they develop on a residential and largely pedestrian campus. When the sky fills with Canada geese heading south on a September evening, honking their hearts out against a bright red sunset, there is no better place to be.

I suppose it is possible to feel isolated on a campus seventy-five miles from the nearest big city, but the advent of social media makes that hard to imagine. As small and rural as my Piedmont window may be, it looks out on a global change of consciousness accelerated by everything from the shopping patterns of millennials to the Twitter feeds of the Trump presidency. My smartphone connects me to a rabbi in Jerusalem protesting the limits placed on her and other women who want to pray at the Western Wall. When I need some visuals of a Hindu funeral for class, YouTube offers me footage of a string of cremations taking place concurrently along the Ganges River in Varanasi.

This sets up a weird tension between the small window of my classroom and the small window of my phone. Which is giving me a better picture of the real world? Are the headlines in my newsfeed truer than the ones in my local newspaper? If I trust what I see on my phone more than what I see out my window, what does it mean to believe that the real world is not where I live?

For the purposes of this book, I choose to trust the classroom first. The phone remains my link to the world beyond my two-stoplight town, but the classroom is all I know well enough to speak truly of it. My shelves are lined with big, smart books about the changing religious landscape of America, the role of religion in global conflict, the mandate for interfaith education in public schools, and the emerging worldviews of the spiritual-but-not-religious. These valuable resources have shaped my thinking and teaching about religion so significantly that they and their authors are listed in the back of this book.

As much as I rely on their work to help me understand the bigger picture, I keep hoping there is room for a book on the smaller picture as well—a far more local one that focuses on the lives of fewer than thirty people at a time, whose truth

1

Religion 101

There is no one alive today who knows enough to say with confidence whether one religion has been greater than all others.

ARNOLD TOYNBEE

Today is the first day of class. Every chair is full. Religion 101 is always full, though I never know what to make of this. Do students sign up because they have heard about the field trips followed by free meals or because they have heard I am an easy grader? Are they here because they want to know more about the religions of the world or because the course meets one of their general education requirements? I never know, but today is the day I have to give them every reason to stay in the class, or they will drop it and shop for something else. How can I convey how important it is that they stay?

When I began teaching this course in the last millennium I billed it as a world tour. "How many of you have been to India?" I asked. No hands went up.

"How about Israel?" Still no hands.

"Saudi Arabia?" One girl raised her hand.

"My dad served in Desert Storm," she said.

"I'd like to hear about that," I said.

Then I told her and the others how this course would take them to all of those countries and more, at least in their imaginations. They would hear the call to prayer from the Great Mosque of Mecca and listen to a cantor sing the Kol Nidre on the eve of Yom Kippur. They would see the inside of the Church of the Holy Sepulchre in Jerusalem and sit in the shade of the Bodhi tree in northeast India where the Buddha achieved enlightenment. By the end of the course, they would be able to tell a stupa from a synagogue, a mandir from a minaret. They would know a few words in Sanskrit, Hebrew, Arabic, and Greek. Those who were religious would learn more about their own faith, and those who were not would learn how other people answer the big questions of human existence: Why are we here? What are we supposed to be doing? When we die, is that it? Whether the students agreed or disagreed with other people's answers to those questions, taking them seriously would help them ask better questions of themselves.

"Where else can you get all of that without a passport?" That was my pitch in the last millennium, when most people thought of world religions as religions that existed somewhere else in the world. Even the textbook conspired with that illusion, supplying glossy photos of Hasidic Jews in Jerusalem and Buddhist monks in Thailand. The VHS tapes I used to keep things lively featured a British guy in a pith helmet who tramped through the jungles of Southeast Asia, the deserts of Egypt, and the slums of Calcutta in search of true Buddhism, Islam, and Hinduism. Although the series had an appealing Mutual of Omaha's *Wild Kingdom* edge to it, the clear message was that world religions were exotic flowers that bloomed elsewhere, among people who were not as fortunate as we.

Even then, the truth was quite different from the perception. By many accounts the first Muslim in America was Estevancio of Azamor, a Moroccan guide for a Spanish expedition in 1528 that landed in Florida.[1] A couple of centuries later, as many as a third of the African slaves in the United States were Muslim. After the Emancipation Proclamation of 1863, they were joined by immigrants from the Middle East, Europe, and India. The earliest mosques in the United States were established in Maine, North Dakota, Michigan, and Indiana between 1915 and 1925.[2]

The first Hindus on American soil may have been the six Asian Indians, employees of the East India Marine Society, who marched in the annual Fourth of July parade in Salem, Massachusetts, in 1851. After Swami Vivekananda addressed the first World Parliament of Religions in Chicago in 1893, he received so many invitations to speak in the United States that he stayed for another two years—founding the Vedanta Society of New York in 1894 and another in San Francisco during his second visit in 1900. The California community built the first Hindu temple in North America in 1906.[3]

Buddhists came during the Gold Rush of the mid-1800s, working not only as miners, but also as loggers, fishermen, farmers, and construction workers who were indispensable to the building of the Central Pacific Railroad. In 1860, 10 percent of the population of California was Chinese. In 1870, the same was true of Montana. By the turn of the century, hundreds of shrines and temples had sprung up along the West Coast and in the Rocky Mountains, including the historic Temple of the Forest Beneath the Clouds in Weaverville, California, built in 1874.[4]

Jews had been living in the United States for 250 years by then. In 1654, when twenty-three Sephardic Jews from Brazil arrived in the Dutch port of New Amsterdam, the first thing they did was to form a congregation for worship. The second thing they did was to apply for permission to create a Jewish burial ground. Although Peter Stuyvesant, the governor of the colony, did not make things easy for them, the port passed to British rule in 1664 and the first synagogue in America was established in the newly named city of New York. By 1820, the largest Jewish community in the United States was in South Carolina, where Jewish men had been given the right to vote and hold office in 1790.[5]

Resistance to these developments took many forms, including legislation. The Chinese Exclusion Act of 1882 prohibited virtually all immigration from China. The Immigration Act of 1917 expanded the banned zone by adding a wide swath of Asia that included India and the Middle East. The Johnson-Reed Act of 1924 added a national-origins quota to the mix, effectively decreasing the immigration of Italians, Jews, and Slavs from Southern and Eastern Europe. The main purpose of the Act, according to the Office of the Historian at the US Department of State, "was to preserve the ideal of American homogeneity."[6]

Repeals of various aspects of these laws followed in 1943 and 1952, with a sweeping revision in 1965. After Lyndon Johnson signed the Immigration Act of 1965 into law at the foot of the Statue of Liberty in October of that year, the United States welcomed a spate of newcomers from Latin America, Asia, Africa, and the Middle East. By 2005, their grandchildren were roughly the same age as the students in my class.

The textbook for Religion 101 had changed by then. The VHS tapes were long retired. If I wanted students to see true Hinduism, Buddhism, Judaism, or Islam, all we had to do was get in the college van and drive seventy-five miles south to Atlanta, where we could visit the North American seat of the Dalai Lama's Tibetan Buddhist monastic lineage or the $10 million mosque near

Georgia Tech. During the unit on Hinduism we had so many choices that I alternated between large and small, taking students to the thirty-acre Bochasanwasi Akshar Purushottam Sanstha (BAPS) temple complex in the suburbs one semester and the homey Vedanta Center of Atlanta the next. Once, on a field trip to the old Hare Krishna Temple near Emory University, several students mistook a statue of the founder for a living person and marveled at how quietly he sat during the entire service.

As hard as I work to keep class interesting, it is the field trips the students remember. To be fair, they are what I remember too—especially the first ones, when I was still finding my way around an Atlanta I did not know existed. Though I had gone to high school and college there and returned from seminary to work at a downtown church in the 1980s, the only religious diversity on my radar involved varieties of Protestants, Catholics, and Jews. I passed many of their landmark buildings every day, almost all of them on Peachtree Road. The Episcopal Cathedral of Saint Philip, the Roman Catholic Cathedral of Christ the King, and Second Ponce de Leon Baptist Church were next-door neighbors. Peachtree Road United Methodist Church was a little farther north; Covenant Presbyterian, Redeemer Lutheran Church, and the Reform Jewish Temple were a little farther south.

I am already in trouble for not naming the other big churches along that stretch, but the point is that none of them was a meditation center, a gurdwara, or a mosque. In the 1960s and 1970s the economic capital was not there for those buildings yet. The communities that would eventually create them were still meeting in homes and storefronts, which made them invisible to people like me—not just physically, but also psychologically. We do not see what we do not expect to see. The first time I passed the

Hindu Temple of Atlanta south of the airport, I thought it was a water park. The first time I passed Al-Farooq Masjid near Georgia Tech I thought it was a Greek Orthodox church. The communities that funded those buildings were two of the earliest to build impressive worship spaces in Atlanta. Neither of them was on Peachtree, though more than one tourist has mistaken the gold domes of the historic Fox Theater on Atlanta's main street for those of a grand mosque.

When I began teaching world religions, I had to relearn the city I had grown up in, not only because it had changed, but because I was changing too. Though I had long been drawn to the study of other religions, I was so surrounded by my own that there was no reason to think very deeply about how the faith of others might affect mine. There was also no pressing need to think about how the exclusive truth claims of my tradition affected people who stood outside of them. I was on the world tour I had advertised to my students, and I was enjoying it very much.

The second year I taught world religions at Piedmont, a student asked to see me before the last day of the drop-add period. When he showed up at the door of my office, he stood there a moment as if he were still deciding whether to come in. Maybe it was the three-foot-tall statue of the Buddha that did it or the framed Arabic calligraphy on the wall. My office has four generous windowsills, each holding objects from one of the religions we study in class, so without even stepping into the room he was faced with a brass Hanukkah menorah; an Ethiopian icon of St. George painted on goat skin; a large statue of the elephant-headed Hindu god Ganesha; and another of Guanyin, a feminine embodiment of compassion in Mahayana Buddhism.

"Are you a Christian?" he asked me.

"I am," I said.

To his credit, he decided to come in. To my relief, he did not ask me what kind of Christian I was, since that is always hard to explain. When I first moved to Clarkesville, where there is still only one Episcopal church in the whole county, people trying to pronounce the name of my denomination sometimes landed on "Espicopal" (rhymes with "despicable"). When I went to the grocery store in my clerical collar, people would sometimes mistake me for a nun. But this young man was not interested in denominational distinctions. After he had taken a seat with his back to the Buddha, he told me he was concerned about the content of my class. He had come to a church-related college for a reason, he said. His faith meant a lot to him, and he did not want to put it at risk.

"If you really are a Christian," he said, "then are you going to help us see what is wrong with these other religions? From what you have said so far it doesn't sound like it, and if that's the case, then I don't think I can stay in the class."

Bees started buzzing inside my head when he said that. I was not angry, exactly. There was nothing belligerent in his tone to warrant that. I was dumbfounded instead, spiritually concussed from my sudden collision with such a solid wall of conviction about what it meant to be Christian. As hard as I had worked to create a course that spotlighted the wisdom of the world's great religions, I had not imagined that someone might take it in order to unplug all of them but one. Yet there he sat—a reminder not only of my short-sightedness but also of a whole different way of being Christian.

I remembered meeting people like him when I was in college. They had fallen in love with Jesus and set out to prove their loyalty by dismissing any truth that did not hinge on him. Their job, as they saw it, was to come up with solid Christian answers to every important question and then to defend those answers against all rivals. When I fell in love with Jesus, I thought that was the only way to do it. Then, after about two weeks of being told I could only attend Bible study with other girls, not boys, and that if I wanted to argue about anything, I should be prepared to offer solid scriptural support for my view, I began yawning from lack of oxygen. I dropped out of Bible study and found another group of Christians, who were more interested in talking about the right questions Jesus asked than in giving the right answers about him. Although I sometimes missed the fevered certainty of the first group, I never missed their constraint. God was too great and the world too wide to allow for so little curiosity.

So, yes, I looked down on Christians who were not like me, including the student who sat in front of me returning the same look. Our standoff reminded me of so many other encounters since my college days: the steely confrontation between true believers, each needing the other to be wrong in order to be right. In this regard, it was difficult to discern what made the confrontations between Christians any different from the confrontations between Christians and people of other faiths.

In the present moment, however, the difference was that I had thirty years on the young man in front of me. He was the college student; I was the teacher. Remembering that, I asked him to tell me a little more about himself, though we both knew where the conversation was going. The Bible was his guide to Christian living, he told me. It said very clearly that Jesus was the only way to God. If the course was not going to support that truth, then he would be forced to drop it. I thanked him for coming and said I hoped I would see him in class on Thursday.

He did, in fact, drop the course. While I was sorry to lose him, he taught me two important things. The first was that my practice of Christianity was pretty specialized. I was used to standing in front of a bunch of Episcopalians, not a classroom that included Jehovah's Witnesses, Missionary Baptists, Seventh-day Adventists, Mormons, and Pentecostals, along with a wide range of Christians from mainline denominations. Semester by semester they reminded me how limited my experience of Christianity really was and what a tiny slice of it I knew well. My full immersion in my own religion was about to take an entirely new turn, and it was going to call for a level of theological humility that I had not practiced in quite some time.

The other thing the student taught me by dropping my class was that I needed better answers to his question. Why *should* someone like him take a course in world religions that highlighted the best and not the worst? Where *were* the Bible verses that supported my point of view? Surely there was something in Christian scripture, history, or tradition that might set someone like him at ease. It was not enough for me to feel certain about the wideness of God's embrace. If I wanted to stay connected to the roots of my tradition, which I did, then it was time for me to make better connections with more traditional Christians, or at least with the sources they hold dear. My alternative was to become one more polarizing Christian who looks down on those who do not love Jesus the way she does.

It was the beginning of my education in teaching world religions, which would have been hard enough in a static world. Since I taught them in a world that was always changing—the media, the headlines, the skyline, the students—my syllabus changed every semester. The one I handed out on my first day of class would be a great embarrassment to me now, with its false confidence and clear parameters. The one I used last semester is fifteen pages long, with dozens of hyperlinks, field-trip opportunities, and elective assignments featuring religious holidays, rituals, art, music, dress, and dance.

The "world tour" speech is gone now, replaced by one that highlights the more practical benefits of religious literacy. Whether students intend to become teachers, nurses, police officers, or businesspeople, I tell them, religious illiteracy is a luxury they can no longer afford. This is a new idea for them—that illiteracy might be a problem in religion as well as English—or that a religion class might have life applications beyond going to church.

A nursing major was the first to break this seal in my class. Three weeks into the unit on Hinduism, she told me she wanted to do her elective on Hindu views of illness and death. "I want to know how to take care of a Hindu patient in the hospital," she said, "and I just realized I don't know." When I was a hospital chaplain in the 1980s I never once thought about that. I did not have to, because I was a Christian chaplain at Georgia Baptist Hospital, where I never met a patient who was not Christian. Now, even in a hospital as small as the one in Habersham County, that would not be the case.

Business majors are more likely to relate to people across desks than bedpans, but they can benefit from knowing how people of different faiths view borrowing and lending money. Education majors need to know where the major holidays of their students fall on the academic calendar, especially the ones that are not on the Christmas–Passover axis of the public-school system. Sports management majors need to know the same thing, especially since the month-long fast of Ramadan can occur during any season of the year. Dietary laws may also affect the sorts of places athletes can and cannot eat while they are on the road. A criminal justice major once told me that he never expected to learn anything in Religion 101 that would help him be a better detective. Then he learned about the ways that people of different faiths treat their dead—including murder victims—and why some families might resist allowing an autopsy that would help law enforcement do its job.

This new emphasis on religious literacy across the professions works well, since even students who are not religious can see the benefit. At the same time, I have read enough student papers to know what most of them will really be working on this semester: their own relationship to the divine. Some may call it "ultimate reality" instead, but their questions will be the same. What is true and what is not? How did they come to believe what they believe? If the bottom drops out, how far will they fall? If there is only one God, why are there so many religions?

What I know and most of them do not yet is that even people who belong to the same religion do not agree about what they mean when they say "God." Some mean a loving daddy, while others mean a cosmic judge. Some see Jesus on a cross and some see him on a white horse with a sharp sword in each hand. Some frankly admit that they do not know what they mean, though they know they ought to—and though they have prayed hard for some clear word from above on those nights when the sound of their own heart scares them half to death.

It is one of the reasons why I never tire of teaching the class and why it never rolls out the same way twice. Every semester brings a new mix of students who will affect each other in ways no one can predict. When the first-generation Bosnian American speaks of his grandfather who died in the war, the cheerleader beside him stops doodling to look at him. When the just-coming-out gay history major lands in the same small group as a just-gone-rogue messianic Jew on the debate team, they both find new best friends.

Maybe these relationships are all that really matter, since it is impossible to teach five great religions in fifteen weeks. I can tinker with the syllabus all I like, but students will still come out blinking at the end, some of them suddenly unable to remember whether Torah goes with Judaism or Islam. Was Jesus born before or after the Buddha? After years of being crushed by this outcome, I now see it as a proper response to the disorientation of Religion 101.

All their lives, most of these students have looked out at the world through Christian glasses. They have learned to describe what they see in Christian terms and not to ask questions about what they cannot see clearly. Now, having tried on some glasses from other traditions—one or two of which have brought troublesome areas of their lives into sharper focus for the first time—they are suddenly aware of how many ways there are to view reality. The lens is not the landscape. It is a way of translating the landscape so that people can walk upright on it, making some sense of what happens to them.

To complicate matters, some students realize for the first time that Catholic lenses are different from Protestant ones, just as Asian lenses are different from Native American ones. Remembering that Torah goes with Judaism is a very minor detail to most of them at this point. They are still trying to get their heads around the fact that God may speak more languages than they ever thought, to far more people than they thought, using different methods than they thought. Either that, or the whole thing is fiction.

I hope that is not the conclusion they reach. As much as I respect their reasons for becoming more spiritual than religious,

I want the young people in my classes to know that religion is more than a source of conflict or a calculated way to stay out of hell. Religions are treasure chests of stories, songs, rituals, and ways of life that have been handed down for millennia—not covered in dust but evolving all the way—so that each new generation has something to choose from when it is time to ask the big questions about life. Where did we come from? Why do bad things happen to good people? Who is my neighbor? Where do we go from here? No one should have to start from scratch with questions like those. Overhearing the answers of the world's great religions can help anyone improve his or her own answers. Without a religion, these questions often do not get asked.

I also want the students to know that while every religion has its villains, each also has its saints. In the quiet backwater of my second-floor cinder-block classroom, I want to give their imaginations something better to work with than what they are getting from the movies and the news—some of the treasures in the chests they have never had any reason to open before. I want them to know about Mohandas Gandhi, Thich Nhat Hanh, Jalāl al-Din Rumi, and Abraham Heschel. I want them to know about the desert fathers and mothers, Teresa of Ávila, Dietrich Bonhoeffer, and Desmond Tutu.

For reasons I have yet to explain to you, I believe this has become my Christian duty. I believe it is the neighborly thing to do, the Christlike thing to do. Part of my ongoing priesthood is to find the bridges between my faith and the faiths of other people, so that those of us who draw water from wells on different sides of the river can still get together from time to time, making the whole area safer for our children.

The students are not my children, but I do want to make the world safer for them. As tired as I get of grading their papers, I never tire of *them*—of trying to find better ways to expand their thinking without blowing their minds; of exposing the lies they have been told about people of other faiths without causing them to distrust their own families of faith; of preparing them for the criticism they will almost surely face if they are vocal about finding anything they admire in faiths other than their own. As often as I have been warned that no one can protect students from the alienating effects of higher education, I still hate to see it happen—as it will in this semester's class, if all goes well.

At the end of the first day of class, I give the students a brief quiz with basic questions about the five religions they are going to study. "You're not supposed to do well on it," I tell them when their faces pucker with anxiety. "If you cannot answer a single question correctly, then this class is exactly where you need to be. Plus, it can be really helpful to clarify what you don't know as well as what you do." I will return these ungraded quizzes to them on the last day of class, so they can see for themselves how far they have come. There will be a few unclaimed quizzes left over—there always are—reminders of the students who set out on this journey but lost heart before the end.

"Be sure to write your name at the top of your quiz," I say when our time is up. Then the students are gone. I gather up the extra syllabi strewn on the long tables. Next I pack up the menorah, the Shiva, the Buddha, the cross, and the Qur'an that have been with me all these years. We have seen a lot, and still we begin again. Heaving my satchel over my shoulder, I wonder what the students will teach me this time. Was it really twenty years ago that I found my way to the Hindu temple in Atlanta for the first time?

Vishnu's Almonds

The God of your understanding is just that: the God of your understanding. What you need is the God just beyond your understanding.

RAMI SHAPIRO

The Hindu Temple of Atlanta was not hard to find. There was no other building like it on Riverdale Road, a busy four-lane highway south of the airport lined with used-car lots, muffler shops, coin laundries, and self-storage units. All you had to do was raise your chin to look above the flat asphalt roofs to the tops of the trees, where the tiered tower of the temple rose like a giant sand castle. The first time I saw it I almost wrenched my neck trying to figure out what such a fantastic building was doing in a place like that.

I had been teaching world religions for about a year by then. The textbook and the VHS tapes were already old news. How could anyone teach a living religion without ever leaving the classroom? When it became clear that a brass statue of Shiva and a British guy in a pith helmet were not going to do it, I started scouting sites for field trips in Atlanta. The Hindu temple was the obvious choice, not only because it was so impressive, but also because it was the only one in Georgia. When the founding members broke ground in 1986, devotees came from Alabama, Tennessee, Florida, and the Carolinas to join the celebration.

Construction was still going on when I visited the first time to do reconnaissance, but the central worship area was finished and had been open for some time. Visitors, including student groups like mine, were welcome seven days a week from 9:00 a.m. until 9:00 p.m., with or without a guide. Since there was not a lot going on, I asked for a guide, which was how I discovered that the names of the deities I had memorized did not match the names on the figures inside. Vishnu had become Balaji. Kali had become Durga. Lakshmi had become Padmavathi.

"The gods have thousands of names," the guide said when I asked him. "The names we use here are familiar in the south." The south of India, he meant. It was the beginning of my education in how many Hinduisms there are, which would eventually wake me up to how many Christianities there are, but not yet. At the moment, my mistake with the names added to my general frustration with Hinduism, which had no founder, no single sacred text, no set pattern of worship, and no central statement of belief. Even the names of the gods changed depending on local custom, along with their images in the temples. In one place the deities had milk-white skin. In another their faces were black as night. How was I supposed to teach that kind of variety in four class sessions? Eventually a swami would offer me a metaphor that worked. "You are thinking of Hinduism as a single shop," he said, "but it is much more like a mall, with shops of every kind under its roof. Some shops are large and popular. Others are small and specialized, yet everyone inside them identifies as Hindu."

This matched what I learned from Huston Smith, the great-godfather of all teachers of world religions, in one of his books on my shelf. Hinduism is the great psychologist of the religions, he wrote. It knows that people are different and offers them different paths to union with the divine. Some choose a scholarly path and others a path of service. Some choose a path of meditation and others a path of devotion. Some devote themselves to Vishnu and some to the Divine Mother. Some shun the worship of deities altogether, striving to realize God in themselves with no decoys. Others mix and match. As baffled as I was by this divine array at first, the apparent limitlessness of the Hindu way was fascinating to me, along with the freedom followers had to find their own path.

Yet this was precisely the problem for some Christians I knew—not just the part about realizing God in the self, but also the part about endorsing more than one way to God. At a seminary where I once taught, I met a professor of Christian evangelism who surprised me by saying that the problem with American Christians was that they were all becoming Hindus. This was apparently the worst thing he could think of to say. "Americans want to pick and choose," he said. "They think they can design their own way instead of following the one that Jesus has already laid out for them." I did not know enough to argue with him then, but the sound of his disdain has never left my ears.

Back at the Hindu Temple, I decided that it was a safe enough place to begin exploring religion beyond the classroom and got back in my car to go home. Two weeks later I returned with a college van full of students and a faculty colleague whom I will call Dr. Acharya. She was a professor of mathematics at the college who stood out in the faculty lineup at graduation every year with her flowing gown from the Indian Institute of Technology in Delhi. I did not know her well, but when I invited her to go on the field trip, she said yes without even checking her calendar. The temple was ninety minutes away from the college and she did not drive, so she jumped at the opportunity to go.

The students were still standing around in the college parking lot when she arrived in an emerald sari with gold threads, her black hair parted straight down the middle and pulled back into a bun. Those who had mastered understanding her accent in order to pass her classes stepped aside to let her through as she headed straight for the front passenger seat of the van. Accepting helping hands from students on both sides, she climbed the two steps and landed in her seat with a great puff of held breath. Someone hauled her carryall in after her. We were ready to go.

Dr. Acharya knew I was Christian, so she staked out her territory early in the ride.

"I have nothing against the Lord Jesus," she said before we had gone a mile. "As a Hindu I love him too, but loving him does not mean I cannot love Lord Vishnu. Do you see?"

"I see," I said. Then we talked about how our classes were going. Once the students had plugged in their earphones or were snoozing with their foreheads pressed against the windows, she told me how much she worried about her grandchildren. As third-generation Indian Americans, she said, they were at risk of losing their religion. She did what she could to remind them of the holidays and the importance of worship, but since she did not live with them, there was only so much she could do. *Huh*, I thought. Christians are not the only ones worried about their grandchildren's faith in a changing world.

When we arrived at the temple an hour and a half later the students woke up and pulled the plugs from their ears.

"Are we there yet?"

"Look at that!"

"What is *that*?"

I was headed to a parking place near the grand staircase to the main entrance when Dr. Acharya pointed to a small door on the ground level instead. "That's the way we go in," she said.

It looked like a stage entrance to me, but she had been there a lot more times than I had. I parked the van, the students piled out, and we all stood looking up at the ornate building that rose high above our heads. When I looked around for Dr. Acharya, I saw her sitting in the van, waiting for someone to notice that she required assistance. The same two students who had helped her into her seat helped her out of it. Then she smoothed her sari, reached back inside the van for her carryall, and started walking toward the door.

"Come," she said. Like ducklings, we all followed her inside. The smell of garam masala was so strong that it made my stomach growl. While Dr. Acharya excused herself to go to the restroom, I turned to a glass booth on my right where the temple manager sat behind a set of sliding windows.

"I called ahead about a class visit," I said.

He nodded and wrote something down on a pad of paper in front of him. Then he pointed to a small room and said something I had to ask him to repeat. "Please leave shoes there," he said again with a lilting accent. "Then walk up." He made a walking motion with the fingers on his right hand to make sure I understood.

While the students were pulling off their shoes and shoving them into cubbyholes, I told them most of what I knew. "This is the only Hindu temple for a couple of hundred miles around. This part was built in 1990. People drive here from Alabama and South Carolina for the biggest festivals. We're here to observe a weekly worship service for one of the major deities. Dr. Acharya said to go on up, and she would meet us inside."

Something had clearly changed since my visit two weeks before. When we reached the doorway of the main hall, the place was full of activity. A priest in an orange robe that left much of his upper body bare was sitting on a carpet with a young couple and a baby. Another priest was deep in one of the several alcoves, waving a lit wick in front of a deity taller than he was. Elsewhere in the room people were doing all kinds of things. Some were saying prayers in front of a statue of Ganesha, while others circled a table with tall stones on it. Some were pressing folded bills through the slot of an offering box in front of the goddess Durga, while others were dipping their fingers into bowls of colorful powder and pressing it into the spot between their eyebrows.

All of a sudden I saw everything through the students' eyes and suffered a little panic attack. Were they ready for this, I wondered? Should I have prepared them better? That would have been difficult to do, since I had only been to one Hindu temple in my life, but still. Voluptuous deities carved from gray stone lined the walls, their arms and legs raised in sacred dance. The air was dense with the smells of softening fruit, burning sandalwood, hot oil, and fresh flowers. The students followed me a little way in and stopped in a clump behind me. Glancing around, I could easily see where the smells were coming from. Butter lamps and sticks of incense burned in front of alcoves containing deities whose necks were draped with garlands of red and yellow flowers. At their feet were mounds of ripening bananas and split coconuts along with bowls of almonds and flower petals. There was nothing anywhere that looked remotely like a church.

When Dr. Acharya finally appeared, she led us over to the

alcove of Padmavathi, a manifestation of the goddess Lakshmi. We were there for a weekly ritual in which priests bathe her, dress her in new clothes, and wreathe her with fresh flowers on behalf of her devotees. Simply to witness the ceremony confers blessing on those who watch, and there were quite a few people there to do that, though it was hardly the only thing going on in the main hall. At least seven deities held places of honor in the room, not counting the nine planetary gods represented by the tall stones on the table.

For most Christians, including me, that many gods takes some getting used to. Never mind for a minute that Christians believe Jesus is one of three Persons in whom God comes to us (which would make perfect sense to a Hindu). The point is that we stop at three. The point is that we have had a lot of practice being around our three, so that they are no longer alarming to us. The fact that some Hindu deities have more than one set of arms and others have the heads of animals makes them appear even stranger to people used to worshipping someone who looks a lot like us.

When I bring the image of Shiva to class on the first day, the students have no frame of reference for what they see. A few know he is the Hindu god of destruction, but that does not help. Why would anyone worship a god who destroys? He is dancing in a ring of fire on the back of a small creature that looks like a child or a dwarf. He has swinging dreadlocks and twice too many arms, some of which are holding things impossible to identify. A cobra uncurls from his top right arm, while another swirls around his waist. This is entirely too many snakes for someone raised on the Garden of Eden story.

When we take the symbols one at a time, however, the image becomes less fearsome. The ring of fire is the eternal cycle of creation and destruction. Dancing inside of it, Shiva reminds the viewer that the god who presides over death clears the way for new life. The creature under his feet is not a child but a demon signifying the ignorance that trips people up and keeps them down. Shiva holds a drum in one of his hands, a flame in another. With his other two hands he makes ancient gestures that mean, "Seek refuge" and "Fear not."

The fact that we need so much help understanding what we are looking at is a lesson in itself. How often do we assume that we know what we are seeing when we see other people practicing their faith? Once, after I published a short essay on the way quantum entanglement (which Einstein called "spooky action at a distance") illumined the concept of divine union, I received a curt letter from a theoretical physicist. "It is not enough for you to think you know what physicists mean when they say something," he wrote. "You need to know what *they* think they mean when they say it."

I have never forgotten this cogent reprimand, which has served me in a great variety of situations. When I think I see a Buddhist worshipping a statue of the Buddha, I yield to the Buddhist when he tells me that he is not worshipping the Buddha but honoring the Buddha's example. When I think I see a Muslim woman constrained by her headscarf, I listen when she tells me how hard she fought to wear it against her family's wishes. As natural as it may be to try to translate everything into my own religious language, I miss a lot when I persist in reducing everything to my own frame of reference.

At the same time, it seems possible that knowing my own language of faith in depth may help me recognize similar depths in other traditions. When I learn that the image of Shiva I have brought to class is called Shiva Nataraja, Lord of the Dance, I cannot help but think of a Christian hymn by the same name.

It was a favorite in the congregations I once served, with a first verse that goes like this:

I danced in the morning
When the world was begun,
And I danced in the moon
And the stars and the sun,
And I came down from heaven
And I danced on the earth,
At Bethlehem
I had my birth.[1]

I doubt that the lyricist, an English songwriter named Sydney Carter, had read the apocryphal *Acts of John.* In that second-century manuscript, which was not on the short list for the New Testament, Jesus commanded his disciples to surround him on the night before he died. After they had circled round him, he danced inside the ring they made, singing a long mystical hymn to which they responded with a chorus of "Amens."[2]

Carter may or may not have known that, but as it turns out he *did* have a statue of Shiva Nataraja on his desk when he wrote the words to his song. For some Christian listeners, this explains why the first verse of his hymn sounds a little pagan to their ears, even after Carter set it to an old Shaker tune. For other Christians, including Carter himself, there is no contradiction. "I see Christ as the incarnation of the piper who is calling us," he wrote in 1974.

He dances that shape and pattern which is at the heart of our reality. By Christ I mean not only Jesus: in other times and places, other planets, there may be other *Lords of the*

Dance. But Jesus is the one I know of first and best. I sing of the dancing pattern in the life and words of Jesus.[3]

The Jesus of the New Testament never dances, I am sorry to say, but that does not stop countless Christians from dancing with him while they sing the refrain they know by heart.

Dance, then, wherever you may be,
I am the Lord of the Dance, said he,
And I'll lead you all, wherever you may be,
and I'll lead you all in the Dance, said he.[4]

I hum the tune to myself when I am back in my office with the image of Shiva on my desk. The longer I look at it, the more I see in it. Though I understand the difference between reincarnation and resurrection, the pattern is familiar to me: there is no new life without destruction. One follows from the other, as both Lords of the Dance know full well.

"Those who try to make their life secure will lose it," Jesus said, "but those who lose their life will keep it." Later he reminded his friends that unless a grain of wheat falls into the earth and dies, it will remain a single grain—but if it dies, it will bear much fruit. Looking at the statue of Shiva, I wonder if an image of the crucifixion would be any less repellant to someone who had not been initiated into the mystery it represents. Is a man hanging on a cross any less frightening than a man dancing in a ring of fire? I have never said this to a student, but I see what the two images have in common. There is no way around the cross or the fire for the faithful who stand in awe of them. Death is the door to new life. No one rises again without first being destroyed.

When I examine the crouched figure under Shiva's right foot, I realize that we all look that small when we are doing everything in our power to avoid being dismantled and made new—when we curl in on ourselves, trying to hang on to things the way they are. Shiva is not killing our too-small souls. He is dancing on us, leaving open the possibility that we might rise up and join the dance too.

As the brass image starts to make sense to me like this, I have to wonder what is going on. Am I beginning to understand it, or am I projecting teachings from my own tradition onto it? At the very least, I am noticing how hard it is to cross the boundary from one set of religious images to another. Rings of fire, hooded cobras, and small bent figures under heavy feet do not put me in a reverent mood. In my religious universe, skies full of angels, descending doves, and bent people standing upright work much better. Those are the symbols that power my sacred stories, or at least the ones that mean the most to me.

But I am getting way ahead of myself here. Back at the temple, on my first field trip, it is time for Padmavathi's bath. First the priests remove her old clothes, which they will give to her devotees. Then they bathe her with rosewater, yogurt, and ghee. The smells mingle as the leftovers fall into a basin at her feet. Her slick skin reflects the light above her head. I have never seen anything like this mix of the sensual and the sacred, with no fireproof ditch between the two. I wish Christians were this comfortable with bodies. The belief that Jesus was fully human does not seem to have reached the level of blessing flesh the way I am watching it being blessed right now. Finally the priests pull the curtain while they dress the goddess in this week's new clothes and drape her neck with fresh flowers.

This will take some time, Dr. Acharya tells me. If we were

devotees of the goddess, we might sit in front of her alcove and chant mantras while we waited for her to reappear. Since we are not, we are free to look around. The students peel off in different directions. A freshman named Bryan goes over to get a closer look at the table of tall stones. Later he will tell me that when he drew near them, he felt such a rush of energy that he knew it was the presence of God. Three basketball players drift toward the statue of Ganesha. There they stand with their hands in their pockets, watching worshippers put burning sticks of incense in a dish of sand in front of the elephant-headed god.

While I am watching them, I see a student named Mariah run past them on her way out the front door. She is a tense girl in her first year of college, with sharp features and a troubled countenance. Walking quickly after her, I catch up with her on the front porch of the temple, where she is standing in the twilight, crying so hard that she cannot answer me when I ask her what is wrong. Finally she catches her breath long enough to tell me.

"They are all so lost, and they don't even know it!" This brings on a fresh round of tears, after which she manages a few more words between tattered breaths. "It is just so sad to me," she says, "seeing people worshipping statues when they could be worshipping Jesus instead." One more sob, followed by one more deep breath. "It just breaks my heart." My heart breaks for her too, but there is no way I can make this better for her, not now in any case. There are other students inside. Even if there were not, it might take hours to help Mariah make sense of what she is feeling and why. I might try to change her mind, which would be a mistake.

"Why don't you stay out here and pray?" I say. "It's a beautiful night. We'll be along soon." I do not know what else to suggest.

The Jesus she loves so much will surely look after her while the rest of us finish up inside.

When I return, Padmavathi's devotees are lining up to face each other in two rows, as if they are waiting for her to step out of her limo and walk the runway in her new clothes. When the priests finally open the curtains, the children in front gasp at the sight of her. Clothed like a queen, she is resplendent in a new red silk sari, with so many garlands of fresh flowers around her neck that her placid face floats above them like the moon.

After the ritual is over, I start fishing in my pocketbook for the keys to the van, but when I look around for Dr. Acharya, she is standing in front of Balaji/Vishnu's alcove saying something to a priest. She has already handed him something she has pulled out of her carryall. Later I will find out it was a yard of saffron silk for the dressing of other deities. When I catch her eye, she motions to me to join her deeper inside Vishnu's shrine.

I gather up all the students I can find, and they follow me inside. We are eager to get a better look at the very large, very imposing image of the deity, who is taller than the tallest basketball player in our group. The problem is that we have forgotten we are in a house of worship, not a wax museum. We are expecting the priest to tell us more about what the statue is made of, why it is black, and what the worship of Vishnu entails, but he does not explain anything. Instead, he begins a sonorous chant and starts tossing flower petals at the deity's feet. A heat wave breaks over me as I realize that Dr. Acharya has asked him to perform a prayer ritual for our group, asking the Lord's blessing on us and on our studies. We have unwittingly crossed over from observation to participation, and there appears to be no way out.

The students and I stand in a semicircle before the deity with our hands clasped in front of us as though we are protecting our private parts. Then the chant ends, and the priest turns toward us with a lit lamp in his hands. None of us knows what to do. Dr. Acharya is at the end of the line where she cannot help us. We stand perfectly still, our faces lighting up one by one as the priest holds the lamp in front of us. When he gets to Dr. Acharya, she cups the flame with her hands and raises her palms to her face. It is a lovely gesture, though I have no idea what it means. Is this how a visitor to an Episcopal church feels watching someone genuflect before entering a pew? Reverence is easy to recognize, even when its meaning is unclear.

The priest sets the lamp on a table, exchanging it for a bowl of liquid and a spoon. This constitutes a crisis, since holding still will no longer suffice. The liquid requires a response that none of us is religiously equipped to make. What started out as a heat wave inside me becomes something much more combustible. There is a colossal pileup on my mental highway, with cars crashing into each other on all sides. My mind careens from the first commandment in Exodus 20 ("You shall have no other gods before me") to the apostle Paul's teaching on idol worship in 1 Corinthians 8 ("For if others see you, who possess knowledge, eating in the temple of an idol, might they not, since their conscience is weak, be encouraged to the point of eating food sacrificed to idols?"). All of my air bags have deployed. The students are looking at me for guidance. Should I stay in my car or get out and direct traffic? *What would Jesus do?*

I decide to stay where I am, dropping my gaze so students will have one less thing to worry about while they decide what *they* will do. As I am waiting for the priest to arrive in front of me, my mind rewinds to a wedding celebration in rural Ethiopia. My husband Ed and I were not invited guests. We were tired hikers with trail dust up to our knees, trying to make ourselves invisible as we walked past the open tent full of happy people. Since we looked like beings from another planet, this turned out to be impossible. A tall smiling man had already separated himself from the wedding party and was walking toward us with two full glasses of a foaming brown beverage in his hands. When he held the glasses out to us, we could see bits of what looked like muddy straw floating in the sluggish bubbles on the surface of the liquid.

Ed and I accepted the drinks with deep bows and profuse thanks, hoping the kind man would then go back to his party. That way we could find a quiet place to pour the liquid out. But no. He stood there still smiling, lifting his hand to his mouth to let us know that we should drink. So we drank. I heard Ed straining the straw out of his first sip with his front teeth while I tried to do the same thing without making as much noise. The drink was a kind of fermented mead. The gummy bubbles stuck to my upper lip. Ed had to swallow several times before he got his down. I opened my throat and let mine fall straight in. Then we thanked the man again, who looked very pleased with us and with himself as he turned back to the wedding party.

When the Hindu priest reaches me with the bowl, I hold out my hands for the liquid. It is not my wedding, but I am still a guest. After I have drunk what seems to be plain water, I raise my eyebrows at Dr. Acharya. Is that it? Are we done? She shakes her head no. Not yet.

On the priest's next round he holds a shiny metal object that looks like a crown over each of our heads. He is careful never to let it touch anyone's hair. He just holds it a couple of inches over one person's head long enough for whatever blessing it holds to come down. Then he lifts it up again and moves on to the next person to do the same thing. Almost everyone is gazing down now. I am not, which is how I know how frozen they all look, as if they are being knighted into an order they never applied to join. Remembering Mariah (who is still out on the porch), I wonder how many of them are going to call their tuition-paying parents when they get home.

After the crown, the priest starts around the circle with whole almonds in his bowl. Thanks to the textbook I recognize this as *prasad*—food that has been offered to the Lord, who is offering it back to us. The surroundings may be strange, but the pattern is familiar. This is what Christians do with bread and wine. We bring them to the altar along with our other offerings. The priest calls the Holy Spirit to be present in them, so that they become the body and blood of Christ for us. Then we take them into ourselves as holy food. I have never been offered almonds at an altar rail, but I know a sacrament when I see one.

Bryan looks the priest in the eyes when he holds out his hands for the almonds, but the other students are disengaging fast. One of the basketball players shakes his head no, while another student steps behind her classmate's back and drops her head. I imagine speech balloons over the priest's head as his face fills with questions. "Why are you here if you do not want the Lord's blessing? Why would anyone refuse Vishnu's almonds?"

When he gets to me, I hold out my hand for the prasad. I know I am standing with one foot in my tradition and the other on unfamiliar ground. There is an alarm going off in the primitive part of my brain, warning me that I am about to be struck by lightning, but I turn away from it toward the God just beyond my understanding. Right before I put the three tear-shaped nuts in my mouth, I thank the Lord for both the blessing of the food and the chance to pray in another tongue. Then the priest moves past me and returns to the altar with most of the almonds still in his bowl. Dr. Acharya is the first to leave the circle, which is how I know the service is over. I am still dazed, thinking back through all of the decisions I have just made and wondering how this will go down with the students.

It was not so bad. Mariah recovered so well that she earned an A in the class, chiefly on the merit of her final project. All of the students had the same assignment: to put their newly acquired knowledge of the world's great religions to work by designing an interfaith chapel for Piedmont College. Some of the plans were brilliant and others were predictable, but none of them touched me the way Mariah's did. I may have embellished it by now, since I have visited it so often in my imagination, but as I remember it her chapel was round, with nothing inside of it but polished floors, walls, and ceilings made entirely of black marble. "There will be no religious symbols or furniture inside," she wrote. "The lighting will be soft and carefully placed, so that no matter where people look, all they will be able to see are each other's faces reflected back at them." The self and the neighbor, I thought, made visible to one another in the dark marble of God.

By the following semester, word had gotten around that you could not pass Dr. Taylor's class if you did not worship idols, but if anything that helped enrollment instead of hurting it. Students seem to be up for anything that promises to relieve the tedium of their education. I think some of them are still waiting for me to come into class one day with a live chicken and a boning knife.

That first field trip opened a whole new folder of questions for me, both as a person and as a teacher of young persons. Is it better to read about a religion in a textbook than to risk actual contact with it? How would I feel if a group of students visited my church and treated the holiest things inside it like oddities? Can anyone who visits a sacred space remain an observer, or does one become a participant simply by entering in? Does taking part in the ritual of another faith automatically make you a traitor to your own?

The most troubling question of all was why my religion seemed so much less gracious than Dr. Acharya's religion did. She seemed to be an exemplar of it, and her hospitality was impeccable. She welcomed all of us to join her at the high altar in her temple without asking what we believed. She enlisted the priest to offer special prayers for us. She did not distance herself from those who snickered. She did not take anyone to task for refusing the prasad. She opened her arms to us from beginning to end. If there were any problems with the visit, they came from the religious worldview of her guests, who had been taught to be very careful about who and what they embraced. I stewed about it all the way home in the van. Why was my crowd so defensive? Who had convinced us that faith was a competitive sport and that only one team could win for all eternity? With an attitude like that, who could blame a neighbor for sensing that Christian love was mostly charitable condescension?

It was not the first time I had felt shame about an aspect of my faith—or envy of an aspect of someone else's—but it was the most acute. What else was I going to notice about my own religious home as I visited the homes of others? There was no telling, but clearly the time had come to find out.

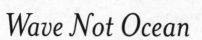

Wave Not Ocean

While living the life of a wave, the wave also lives the life of water. It would be sad if the wave did not know that it is water.

THICH NHAT HANH

What do you mean when you say "God"?

The question takes students aback, since most of them assume that they all mean the same thing. God is God, right? But all of a sudden they are not so sure. I ask them to write their answers on index cards. A great silence settles over the room. Several minutes later, when I ask who needs more time, half a dozen hands go up. The students who have finished thinking about God are checking messages on their phones.

"Don't sign your name," I say when everyone is done. Then I collect the cards, promising to type the answers on a single page of paper so they can read each other's definitions the next time we meet. Later that night I am freshly struck by how fluid a solid-sounding word can be.

Naming God creates God.

God is the alpha and omega, the beginning and the end.

God is anything that is served by humans and worshipped by humans.

God is the embodiment of absolute love, wisdom, and temperance.

God is a fatherlike figure who does not take part in the world.

God is a possibility one can choose to seize or abandon.

God is Abba, daddy, a lap to climb in and cry.

God is a big white guy in the sky.

God is my road, my food, my shelter, and my goal.

God is not the proverbial ear that attracts our stray thoughts and pleas.

Mostly what I know about God is how little I really know about God.

What does any of us mean when we say "God"? We use the word as if it were made of steel girders instead of silk netting, but when we compare what we have caught with it, the divine array confounds—even in a class of twenty-five undergraduates. How much more when we press the word into service for discussion among people of many faiths? The word will not work at all when we come to our study of Buddhism.

The Buddha's teachings never mention God, at least not in the capitalized form that monotheists use. Buddhism's founder, Siddhartha Gautama, grew up in a world of small-*g* gods, but by the time he was a young man he realized that all the gods combined could not bring human suffering to an end. After his enlightenment, he laid out a path to peace that did not involve divine mediators. Instead, he asked people to take responsibility for the working of their own minds. Their desire for pain-free lives was a real problem, he said, since life is never pain-free. The sooner they learned to accept the human condition with equanimity, the sooner their suffering would end—not their pain, but their suffering—since suffering is so often a measure of how much we want things to be different from the way they are.

Contrary to popular opinion, the Buddha never claimed to be God. He never denied the existence of God, either, though there is really nothing for a capital-*G* God to do in his teachings. The things that happen to us are the natural consequences of our actions, and no one can relieve us of them. If we do not like what is happening, it is up to us to change. No one is watching over us to punish or reward us. Enlightenment is its own reward, the peace that passes all understanding. If we want something to do while we are learning to let go of our demands about the way life ought to be, we can devote ourselves to relieving the suffering of others.

As the textbook says, Buddhism is not about God but about the teachings of a man, which raises an interesting question for students in Religion 101. Can you have a religion without a God? If you can, then what takes God's place? How do Buddhists manage without a deity to run the world, forgive sin, punish evil, and grant eternal life?

The more interesting question to me—one I do not take up with the students—is why I am drawn to a tradition so different from my own. Christianity and Buddhism both recognize the centrality of suffering in human life. Both stress compassion.

Both seek lasting peace. Beyond that, they could not see things more differently. The Buddha shows his followers how to achieve salvation. Jesus achieves it for his. The Buddha says the problem is ignorance. Jesus says it is sin. The Buddha says the self is impermanent. Jesus says it is destined for eternal life. I am pretty sure these two teachers could stay up all night talking, but their followers are left with two distinct views of what it means to be human. So why do they both work for me?

One of my favorite authors, Paul Knitter, has written a book called *Without Buddha I Could Not Be a Christian*. In it, he describes the "double-belonging" that led him to become a more committed Christian at the same time that it led him to become a more devoted member of a Tibetan Buddhist community in the United States. When one of his students at Union Seminary in New York asked him if this was "spiritual sleeping around," Knitter took the question seriously. His core identity is Christian, he explained, but it is an identity that flourishes only through mixing it up with others.

Well, that's true, I thought, counting how many other religions Christians mixed it up with during their early years—not just Judaism, but also Samaritanism, Zoroastrianism, and Greco-Roman, Egyptian, and Syrian religions. When Islam arrived in the seventh century, it changed the way Christians thought about their religious images. During that same century, manuscripts blending Buddhist, Taoist, and Christian teachings were being written in China under the influence of a Syriac monk named Alopen.[1] In all of these ways and more, Christian teaching has flourished from its mingling with other religious teachings.

"The more deeply one sinks into one's own religious truth," Knitter says, "the more broadly one can appreciate and learn from other truths."[2]

That has been true for me, both as a teacher and as a spiritual seeker. Unlike the young man bent on keeping his Christian faith uncontested and pure, I have gained insight every time I have put mine to the test. Sometimes the results are distressing, as when I find the silence of the meditation bench more healing than the words of my favorite psalms, or when I take greater refuge in the Buddhist concept of impermanence than in the Christian assurance of eternal life. Yet this is how I have discovered that I am Christian to the core. However many other religious languages I learn, I dream in Christian. However much I learn from other spiritual teachers, it is Jesus I come home to at night.

One of the quietest revolutions in Religion 101 follows a student's recognition that he or she has a worldview, a particular way of viewing reality that is not the only way. A worldview is a wave, but not the entire ocean. Sometimes I bring a globe to class to make the point, since it is easier to identify a physical position than a philosophical one. The globe is a nice big one on a wooden stand. When I put it on my desk it is taller than I am, with the North Pole pointing up and the South Pole pointing down. My country is near the top where it is supposed to be. All is right with the world.

When the students are settled in their seats, I say we are going to talk about the difference between Eastern and Western worldviews. I spin the globe laterally while I am talking so that it looks just like the Universal Studios logo they see at the movies. Then I tip it upside down. "Are you okay with that?" I ask them, once Australia is on top and Canada is at the bottom. "Or did that just make your stomach do a little flip?"

None of us knows we have "a worldview" until we see the world from a new angle. If we are used to seeing ourselves on top, we may feel oddly combative the first time we see someone else up there. We may forget that the reason we are on top is because people like us made the maps. Before Europeans used the North Star to decide which way was up, the worldview of the East was dominant. That is where the word "orientation" comes from: the earth was once oriented toward the Orient. Religions may not be as solid as landmasses, but the same feeling of vertigo can overtake you when you see reality from another angle for the first time—especially if the new view happens to make sense.

A few weeks after the field trip to the Hindu Temple, a small group of students and I are driving up and down Briarcliff Road trying to find Drepung Loseling Monastery in Atlanta. According to the website, it is the North American seat of the Tibetan Buddhist lineage to which the Dalai Lama belongs. Since it is also an affiliate of Emory University, the monk who picked up the telephone earlier in the semester assured me that students were welcome at the Tuesday night public lecture. If that is the case, why is the place so hard to find?

I know we are close, but there is nothing to indicate the presence of a Buddhist monastery nearby. I was hoping for clear signage or at least a Tibetan flag, but the only sign in front of the bunkerlike complex at 2531 Briarcliff Road advertises how many square feet of office space are available for rent. Since the street number on the sign matches the one on the Post-it stuck to my dashboard, I aim the van at the driveway like Harry Potter aiming for platform 9¾ at King's Cross Station the first time he went to Hogwarts. After I find a parking space behind the office buildings, the students get out and stretch.

"Where are we?" one of them asks.

"I wish I knew," I say. Then I start searching for the monastery

on foot with the students trailing behind me like puppies. Sometimes I worry that their trust in me is misplaced.

Bryan, the student who had such a strong experience at the
Hindu Temple, walks beside me reading the nameplates on the
identical office doors. One belongs to an orthodontist, the next
to an attorney. We pass the offices of a travel agent, an accoun-
tant, and a massage therapist before we come to—a Tibetan
Buddhist monastery! Or at least the teaching and meditation
center of one.

The room we step into looks more like a library or a shop,
with bookshelves lining the walls and a shoe rack by the door.
After the students have taken off their boots and sneakers, they
drift off in different directions to investigate. A table in the middle of the room holds the model of a proposed new monastery
complex. The bookshelves are full of CDs, T-shirts, "Free Tibet"
bumper stickers, and incense holders. Bryan heads straight for
the rack of Buddhist prayer beads. About twenty other people
are milling around the room talking, sipping tea, adding their
names to sign-up sheets on a clipboard. There are more women
than men. Some wear yoga pants and others wear jeans. None
wear orange robes. They look a lot like our group, only older.

"Where are the monks?" asks a curly-headed sophomore
named Spencer. During the first week of Religion 101 he de-
clared himself a Buddhist. Since I was too green to know better,
I believed him, feeling chastened when he corrected my pronunciation of Thich Nhat Hanh's name in class.

"I think you mean 'Thay,'" Spencer said right there in front
of everyone.

"I beg your pardon?" I said.

"His name is Thay Nhat Hanh," Spencer said.

"That's news to me," I said.

After class I looked it up and discovered that *thay* is the Vietnamese term for "teacher" or "master." Since I had not yet learned to let students teach me anything—at least not willingly or with any kind of grace—I pointed out the difference between a surname and an honorific at the beginning of the next class.

"Fine," Spencer said. "I just heard it on a tape." Though his Buddhism has turned out to be more aspirational than actual, he is right that there is not a monk in sight at the monastery. Then again, the lecture has not started yet. From where we stand in the bookstore area, we can see into the teaching hall where people are already sitting down on fat black cushions or claiming one of the folding chairs in the back.

The hall is tiny compared to the Hindu Temple, though still plenty dazzling to Western eyes. At the far end of the room stands a large altar flanked by a pair of wooden thrones covered with colorful silk brocade. A framed portrait of the Dalai Lama rests on one of the thrones. The other throne is empty. In between them, a large golden statue of the Buddha sits between images of Padmasambhava, the Indian teacher who brought Buddhism to Tibet, and Green Tara, an embodiment of the divine feminine. There are smaller statues of other teachers and bodhisattvas clustered in threes on either side of them, with ancient-looking books stacked in shelves over their heads and bronze offering bowls lined up on a ledge below them.

There had been a great deal of discussion back at Piedmont about what students would and would not be expected to do in such a room. Since the only religious world most of them knew was Christian, they assumed that the Buddhists were going to try to convert them. One had checked to make sure he would not be asked to bow down to the Buddha. Another had asked for permission to leave the room if she became uncomfortable.

Remembering the scene on the front porch of the Hindu Temple, I said, "Yes, of course," hoping there would be no need for an exit strategy this time.

The dharma hall is beginning to fill up. I tell the students they had better find a place to sit quickly, or they will be stuck on a cushion in the front row. Most enter the hall as if they are going through airport customs in a strange country. Spencer chooses a cushion nearest the wall. Bryan chooses one in front of the empty throne. I settle in a folding chair two rows behind him, watching the other students find their own zones of safety.

A few moments later a volunteer welcomes us and goes over dharma-hall etiquette. No placing of sacred texts on the floor. No pointing of the soles of the feet toward the altar. If you have to leave, leave quietly, without turning your back on the teacher. After the donation basket has been passed around, the regular members of the community stand with their hands pressed together and bow as the teacher enters the room.

"It's like curtseying to the queen," I said in the van on the way down here. "It doesn't make you a Buddhist, I promise." Some of the students bob their heads a little bit, but most are too busy looking at the teacher, who *is* wearing orange robes. He bows to us in return, sits down on a cushion behind a small teaching desk, and clips a microphone to the crimson part of his robe. First he chants something in another language that the regulars chant with him. Then we sit in silent meditation for five minutes before he begins his talk. Since I did not know this part was going to happen, I hope the students know it does not constitute worship.

The monk has to clear his throat a few times before he can get a sentence out without croaking. Maybe it is the pollen, or

maybe it was all that chanting. Then he has to move his microphone around on his robe a couple of times when people in the
back of the hall say they cannot hear. After taking a sip of the
hot tea someone places in front of him, he finally gets down to
business. His topic for the evening is "Cultivating Happiness."

Have we ever noticed, he asks, how quickly our unhappiness
with not being in a relationship turns into our unhappiness
with our new relationship? Have we ever noticed how soon our
unhappiness with not having a job turns into our unhappiness
with the job we finally get? In no more than four sentences he
has made his point: our unhappiness is not dependent on our
circumstances, which are always changing. Tapping his temple
with the fingers of his right hand, he tells us that our unhappiness is a product of our own minds, as we persist in locating
the source of all our problems "out there" instead of "in here."
While we spin our wheels trying to control things beyond our
control, we ignore the one thing that is within our power to
change: our way of seeing things.

When the monk takes another sip of tea, Bryan turns his
head around, so I can see his face—eyes wide, eyebrows up—
mouthing words in a big way so I can get what he is saying.

"This is just about life," he mouths, making his eyes even
wider.

This is just about life. When he says it, I know this is what
draws me to the Buddhist way. This way is not about God. It
is not about gaining converts or opposing other ways. It is
"just" about life, with an open offer of methods for living more
mindfully to anyone who would like to try them out and decide whether they are useful or not. This is another significant
difference between the Buddhist way and the Christian way. In
my way, belief is essential—especially belief in things that are

hard to believe. In the Buddhist way, belief is optional. Try it and see, the Buddha says. Walk the way for a while and decide for yourself what is true. This invitation is thrilling to me. By comparison, my own tradition seems to have much less confidence in my ability to decide anything for myself. Or perhaps it has less confidence in its ability to withstand this kind of scrutiny?

On the day I bring singing bowls to class I know no one will remember a word I say. The bowls are far too interesting— meditation aids made from resonant metals in many shapes and sizes, each tuned to its own key. In Tibetan Buddhist teaching, the different keys speak to the different chakras, or energy centers, of the human body. With a little practice you can learn how to run a wooden striker around the rim of a bowl, so that it produces its own singular song: a faint hum that builds to a thrum that can make the hairs on your arm stand up. One bowl speaks to the crown of the head. One speaks to the heart. Another speaks to the base of the spine. There are seven chakras in all, and I have brought twice that many bowls to class. The students are all over them, coaching each other on how to hold the strikers, but no one knows which bowl is tuned to which chakra yet.

"Listen for the one you like best," I tell the students, "and listen for the one that makes you crazy." While they are making the bowls sing, I take roll, matching the names in my grade book to the students in front of me. There is one I am worried about, a young man from out of state who is all but mute in class. Like many of his peers he has come to Piedmont to play sports, though his family is farther away than most. I am worried about him because he is not turning in his homework assignments and he never speaks to anyone, including me.

While the others are busy passing the bowls around, clamping their hands over their ears when someone loses control of the striker and makes a bowl shriek, he sits looking at his bowl as if it were alive. He does not run the striker around the rim of the bowl. He uses it to tap the bowl gently on the side instead. Then he brings the bowl to his ear and holds it there until the sound has completely died away. He does this over and over again, his eyes shifting to softer focus every time.

"What do you think?" I ask him, leaning a little closer so I can hear the sound too. He smells like rain.

"I think this bowl might be speaking to me," he says. "What chakra did you say it was?"

I turn the bowl over and look at the small sticker on the bottom.

"Heart chakra," I say. He nods as if he already knew.

For many years I began the unit on Buddhism by writing a quote from the Buddha on the board: "Believe nothing, no matter where you read it or who said it, no matter if I have said it, unless it agrees with your own reason and your own common sense." Then I found the saying listed on fakebuddhaquotes .com. That was a bit of a blow. But even if the Buddha never said it, it still led me back to something Jesus said—not once but in many ways—when someone tried to get a definitive answer out of him.

When a man asked him what he had to do to inherit eternal life, Jesus said, "What is written in the law? What do you read there?" On another occasion, when someone asked him if it was lawful to pay taxes to the emperor or not, Jesus said, "Why are you putting me to the test?" Then he asked to see a coin. When someone showed him a coin with Caesar's head on it, Jesus said, "Whose head is this, and whose title?"

As much as Christians regard Jesus as the answer man, he sounds a lot more like the question man to me.

"Why do you see the speck in your neighbor's eye, but do not notice the log in your own eye?"

"Can any of you by worrying add a single hour to your span of life?"

"Which of these three, do you think, was a neighbor to the man who fell into the hands of the robbers?"

"For who is greater, the one who is at the table or the one who serves?"

"Do you want to be made well?"

Jesus seems to know more about the way of transformation than many of his followers do. If someone wants to learn more about God, he implies, it will involve more than believing someone else's answers. It will involve thinking deeply about the questions you are asking and why. Then it will involve acting on the answers you come up with in order to discover what is true.

Back in the teaching hall, the teacher is wrapping up his talk with another brief period of meditation. Later Bryan will tell me what happened to him during this, his first attempt. He did everything right, he said. First, he paid attention to his posture. Then he focused on his breathing, letting it go all the way from his nose down to his feet and back up again—which was when he noticed a deep warmth moving up one of his legs.

"I can't believe this!" he thought to himself. "Here I am meditating for the first time in my life, and I am being given a taste of enlightenment!" Then he opened his eyes to see that the person next to him had spilled her coffee, which was wicking up the left leg of his jeans.

I saved Bryan's field trip report, along with one written by a young man who had been particularly on guard. "There may have been some rituals and ceremonies that I was not sure I wanted to take part in," the wary student wrote afterward, "but when we arrived it was different." To his surprise, he was able to clear his mind during the meditation periods, reaching a place of calm that was new for him. "The whole experience made me think about changing my perspective on what is going on in my life," he wrote. "Not about changing my religion, but the way that I look at things. This may be what we have been learning in class about different worldviews, but I did not understand the concept until I saw it firsthand at the monastery."

That is the silent revolution, and it has taken place inside me too. Through the years I have spent dozens of hours in the presence of Tibetan lamas who have spoken directly to my condition. Their talks have been as meaningful to me as anything I have heard from teachers in my own tradition, though the Tibetans and I speak different languages and they do not speak of God. What can this mean? Since I know how the Dalai Lama handles people who want to convert, I am pretty sure it does not mean I am being called to become a Tibetan Buddhist.

In a book called *Acts of Faith*, author and activist Eboo Patel tells a story about the time he and his friend Kevin were granted an audience with the Dalai Lama in Dharamsala, India. After His Holiness commented on a small empty bowl Kevin wore on a chain around his neck, Kevin told the Dalai Lama how many years he had spent studying the Buddhist concept of emptiness, which seemed to have a lot in common with the Jewish concept of *ayin*.

"You are a Jew?" the Dalai Lama asked him. When Kevin said yes, His Holiness said, "Judaism and Buddhism are very much alike. You should learn more about both and become a better Jew."[3]

I envy that. My tradition has a hard time blessing strong bonds to other traditions, especially those whose truths run counter to our own. We like people to make a conscious choice for Christ and then stay on the road they have chosen, inviting other people to join them as persuasively as they can. It is difficult to imagine a Christian minister talking to a Buddhist who has spent years studying a Christian concept and then telling him to go become a better Buddhist. In some circles, that would constitute a failure on the minister's part, a missed opportunity to save a soul. This is another way in which Buddhism and Christianity differ. Both are evangelistic—what else is a Buddhist mission doing in a suburb of Atlanta?—but the Buddhists seem to understand what Gandhi meant by the "evangelism of the rose." Distressed by the missionary tactics of Christians in his country, he reminded them that a rose does not have to preach. It simply spreads its fragrance, allowing people to respond as they will.

By that definition, I have responded to the fragrance of Buddhism, and it is making me a little anxious—not as anxious as I felt in Vishnu's alcove at the Hindu Temple, but anxious enough to wonder if my attraction to other traditions makes Jesus mad. For most of my Christian life I have been taught that God is a jealous God. In seminary I studied the Hebrew prophets, who use the word "whore" a lot for people who flirt with other gods.

Jesus never used that shorthand, but he did seem forlorn when the people he invited to follow him went in another direction. At this late date it is sometimes hard for me to separate what he said from what the first preachers in my life said he said, but I would be leaving something important out of this book if I did not own up to a palpable fear that grabbed me the first few times my envy of another tradition drew me over to smell someone else's rose. The fear was laced with flames and pitchforks.

Holy Envy

Before I read Gandhi I couldn't see what difference
Jesus made.

ANDREW YOUNG

Early in my tenure at Piedmont, a student who had taken
Religion 101 with me decided to become a Jew. As anyone
who has tried it knows, this is not the same as deciding to become a Christian. Judaism actively discourages converts, since
a person does not need to be Jewish in order to be righteous in
God's eyes. Why take on so many extra responsibilities if you
are fine with God the way you are?

The Piedmont student, whom I will call Natalie, persisted.
She dug into her Jewish studies the same way she dug into her
college studies, with focused drive and intelligence. After she
had met all the requirements, she chose a Jewish name and set a
date for her conversion ceremony at the Reform temple nearest
Piedmont, which was still more than an hour away. I sat in the
congregation with one of her other professors while she gave a
speech about the lessons she had learned and thanked everyone
for helping her. Then the rabbi called Natalie by her new name,

placed a large Torah scroll in her arms, and welcomed her to the
Congregation Children of Israel.

I sat there feeling very happy for her, but also a little jumpy—
not because Natalie had become a Jew, but because it was possible that Religion 101 had played a part in her decision and that
was not in the course plan. I was focused on teaching the basics
of five major world religions, not helping students decide which
one was right for them, yet that was clearly what a number of
them were doing. Another student decided to be baptized for the
first time after a class discussion on the difference between in-
fant and believer's baptisms. Another got a tattoo of a yin-yang
symbol on her forearm during the unit on Chinese traditions.
When she showed it to me after class one day, she asked if I could
steer her toward the nearest Taoist church.

These students were the exception, not the rule, but they reminded me that there is more than one way to respond to religious pluralism. The Christian majority may have been raised to
ignore the truth claims of other religions, but others are strongly
affected by what they learn. Some, like Natalie, make a conscious
decision to convert, either to another world faith or to another
branch of the one they grew up in. There is an Orthodox Christian church eighteen miles from Piedmont that began with some
local Protestants hungry for a richer worship experience. Now
they worship in a building with three gold onion domes on top
of it instead of a white steeple with a cross.

These days, when I offer students a list of options they may
check to describe their religious identity ("Mark as many as apply"), the "spiritual but not religious" option gets a lot of checks.
I know how critical some of my religious friends are about this
designation, which they characterize as shallow, self-serving,
and socially disengaged. Since that describes more than a few

people who are still warming pews, it is hard to understand why the spiritual seeking of one group is less honorable than the other. Is it because one helps pay the utility bills and the other does not?

Based on the young people I know best, more and more of them identify as spiritual but not religious because it is easier than trying to reconcile the teachings of their faith with their affection for their non-Christian friends. According to the teachings they have received in church, their friends are not all right the way they are. Unless they become Christian, God will not allow them to enter heaven. Instead, they will roast in hell for all eternity for refusing to accept Jesus as their Lord. This does not make any more sense to some young people than the teaching that they must choose between the account of creation in the Bible and the one their biology teacher has laid out for them.

These are only a few of the serious questions they have that no one in their churches wants to talk about with them. They want more from their communities of faith than a new music leader, a youth pledge card, and the assurance that they can wear jeans to church. So of course they stop doodling in class when they discover a religion that does not require belief in God or one whose followers believe God is equally present to those of all faiths. The idea that karma might explain the apparent injustice of the universe appeals to some of them, along with the idea that right action might be more important to God than right belief.

All of these teachings caught my attention when I first learned them too. They were as yet unimagined ways of viewing the relationship between the human and the divine, and once I encountered them, I could not let them go. As this book aims to describe, it took me a while to understand that finding these things attractive did not mean it was time for me to convert or—

conversely—to start making a quilt of spiritual bits and pieces with no strong center. The third possibility was to let my attraction to other teachings transform my love for my own.

The first time I heard the phrase "holy envy" I knew it was an improvement over the plain old envy I felt while studying other faiths. When the Jewish Sabbath came up in class, I wanted it. Why did Christians ever let it go? When we watched a film of the God-intoxicated Sufis spinning, I wanted that too. The best my tradition could offer me during worship was kneeling to pray and standing to sing. My spiritual covetousness extended to the inclusiveness of Hinduism, the nonviolence of Buddhism, the prayer life of Islam, and the sacred debate of Judaism. Of course this list displays all the symptoms of my condition. It is simplistic, idealistic, overgeneralized, and full of my own projections. It tells you as much about what I find wanting in my own tradition as it does about what I find desirable in another. This gets to the heart of the problem: with plain old envy, my own tradition always comes up wanting. The grass is always greener in the tradition next door.

I know my Christian pasture so well. I know where the briars are along with the piles of manure. I also know where the springs of living water are, but when I look over the fence at the neighbor's spread, it looks so flawless, so unblemished and perfectly tended, at least from where I stand. From a distance it is easy to forget that every pasture has its turds and stickers along with its deep wells and beds of clover. So when I look longingly at my neighbor's faith, am I really looking for greener pastures, or am I simply trying to make peace with the realities of my own?

When I finally take time to find out where the phrase "holy envy" comes from, I trace it back to a biblical scholar named Krister Stendahl. I remember him from my years at Yale Divinity School, when he was the dean of Harvard Divinity School—a tall, Scandinavian man with a stiff neck and a head of wavy hair. He was such a friend to the women students in his school, many of whom were not eligible for ordination in their churches at that time, that they called him "Sister Krister."

Several years after his tenure as dean was over, Stendahl was elected the Bishop of Stockholm and returned home to Sweden. He had only been in place about a year when he became aware of mounting opposition to a new Mormon temple opening in the summer of 1985. The antipathy was odd in some ways, since Sweden had a long history of welcoming religious strangers even then. It was predictable in other ways, since new religious buildings often cause more anxiety than new religious neighbors do—especially if their buildings are bigger and better looking than yours. The Stockholm temple was designed by Swedish architect John Sjöström with a floor area of more than 16,000 square feet and situated in a leafy suburb of the city.

At a press conference prior to the dedication of the building, Stendahl aimed to defuse tension by proposing three rules of religious understanding, which have by now made the rounds more often than any of his scholarly work on the apostle Paul. Here is the most common version of what he said:

1. When trying to understand another religion, you should ask the adherents of that religion and not its enemies.
2. Don't compare your best to their worst.
3. Leave room for holy envy.

No one is positive what he meant by number three, but Stendahl soon acted on it in ways that required holy courage. As a

Lutheran, he found much to envy in the Mormon practice of vicarious baptism, by which a living Latter-day Saint chooses to be baptized on behalf of a person who has died without completing this requirement for entering God's kingdom. The practice provoked public outrage in the 1990s, when some members of the LDS Church bypassed the rules and submitted the names of Holocaust victims for baptism. Church officials responded by promising to remove those names from its genealogy records. They also clarified that church teachings do not include coercing dead people to become Mormons.

The way it was explained to me, the dead person still gets a choice. When someone on earth is baptized in his or her name, the deceased—who is by now living in the spirit world awaiting Jesus's resurrection from the dead—receives one last chance to say yes to the gospel. Those who are baptized by proxy may refuse, even from beyond the grave, but not without recognizing that someone on the other side has gone to great lengths to include them among the saints.

Since Lutherans have historically shied away from Catholic teachings about how the living might benefit the dead, Stendahl had nothing like vicarious baptism in his own tradition. Yet he saw value in it and proceeded to envy it across the fence. He even went public with his scholarship on the subject, appearing in a Mormon video on vicarious baptism and contributing an article to the *Encyclopedia of Mormonism*. At the moment I cannot think of a parallel in my own tradition for such a gesture. Perhaps if the archbishop of Canterbury went on record as envying the Quaker practice of silent meetings?

Stendahl's decision to stand with the Mormon minority in Stockholm was about more than his interest in the afterlife, however. "In the eyes of God, we are all minorities," he told a

reporter shortly before his death in 2008. "That's a rude awakening for many Christians, who have never come to grips with the
pluralism of the world."[1]

From my limited perspective in a small college classroom, I
believe that increasing numbers of young Christians *are* coming
to grips with pluralism—embracing it, even—though they are
getting very little help from their elders as they think through
what it means to be a person of faith in community with people
of other (and no) faiths. No preacher has suggested to them that
today's Good Samaritan might be a Good Muslim or a Good
Humanist. No Confirmation class teacher has taught them that
the Golden Rule includes honoring the neighbor's religion as
they would have the neighbor honor theirs.

Come to think of it, I do know one preacher who tried something like that—from the pulpit of a cathedral in a major city,
no less. I do not remember what the subject of her sermon was,
only the response to it. She must have suggested that the Christian way was one among many ways to God (a wave and not the
ocean), because afterward a man came up to her and said, "If
God isn't partial to Christianity, then what am I doing here?"

I wish ordinary Christians took exams, so I could put that
question on the final. As natural as it may be to want to play on
the winning team, the wish to secure divine favoritism strikes
me as the worst possible reason to practice any religion. If the
man who asked that question could not think of a dozen better
reasons to be a Christian than that, then what, indeed, was he
doing there?

An old story is told about Rabia of Basra, an eighth-century
Sufi mystic who was seen running through the streets of her
city one day carrying a torch in one hand and a bucket of water
in the other. When someone asked her what she was doing, she

said she wanted to burn down the rewards of paradise with the torch and put out the fires of hell with the water, because both blocked the way to God. "O, Allah," Rabia prayed, "if I worship You for fear of Hell, burn me in Hell, and if I worship You in hope of Paradise, exclude me from Paradise. But if I worship You for Your Own sake, grudge me not Your everlasting Beauty."[2]

In Christian tradition this comes under the heading of unconditional love, though it is usually understood as the kind of love God exercises toward humans instead of the other way around. Now, thanks to a Muslim mystic from Iraq, I have a new way of understanding what it means to love God unconditionally. Whenever I am tempted to act from fear of divine punishment or hope of divine reward, Rabia leans over from her religion into mine and empties a bucket of water on my head.

This, I believe, is how holy envy is meant to work. When students study the Five Pillars of Islam, they linger over the five daily prayers. "People actually stop what they are doing to pray five times a day? They do it wherever they are, even if other people can see them?" This astonishes students who may bow their heads before meals or kneel by their beds at night, but who have never imagined what it would take to ask for time off from work to say their midday prayers or to unfurl a prayer rug at the stadium at sundown to say their evening ones.

Devout Christians struggle with the fact that devout Muslims pray more than they do. They might not call it "holy envy," but it leads more than a few of them to take their own prayer lives more seriously. A Christian student who has never heard of the season of Lent decides to try it this year. It will be her Ramadan, she says. A Muslim student who stopped praying when he came to college says he is getting an app for his phone that will go off five times a day. Maybe all he will do is turn it off, he says, but at least he will know what time it is.

I still remember a Methodist pastor who took the class one fall. Joel was a "nontraditional student," which is academic code for someone who comes to college later in life. I am not sure he ever told me the story of how he came to Georgia from Puerto Rico, but the regional bishop recognized his gifts for ministry and put him in charge of a small congregation before he had earned a college degree. When Joel received a scholarship to Piedmont, he wowed his teachers by carrying a full load at school while he kept his full-time job. When he stopped by my office to say hello with his wife and children in tow, it seemed clear that he was doing as good a job of loving them as he was doing with everything else. He never missed Religion 101 unless one of his church members was being rushed to the hospital or he had a funeral to do.

Joel went on all of the field trips, including one to a large masjid for Friday afternoon prayer. Since Friday is the day Muslims gather for public worship, the service typically draws a large crowd, and this Friday was no exception. More than once during the sermon, the ushers walked among us motioning us to move closer together, so more people could find places to sit. By the time everyone stood up at the end of the service to perform their prostrations, Joel was off to the side with the rest of the students watching three or four hundred people touch their heads to the floor in unison. In the van on the way home, he was very quiet.

"What are you thinking?" I asked him.

"I am thinking about how many people were there," he said, "compared to how many people are in my church on Sunday morning. What is the difference? What makes the difference? That is what I am thinking about." The last time I checked, Joel was a fully ordained elder with a new congregation under his care.

The more I explored the concept of holy envy, the more kinds of religious envy I discovered—and not all of them holy. When I first began teaching Religion 101, my envy took the form of spiritual shoplifting. When I saw something I liked in another tradition, I helped myself: Tibetan singing bowls, Hindu deities, necklaces strung with Zuni fetishes, Muslim prayer rugs. I paid handsomely for all of these things. My desire to possess them stemmed from a genuine wish to draw closer to their original owners, but when I survey the objects on the windowsills in my office—a nineteenth-century spice box made of sterling silver once used for the Jewish prayer service that ends the Sabbath, a splendid wooden Buddha covered with gold leaf from an antique shop in Bangkok, a rare set of Muslim prayer beads from Morocco made from amber—I feel more than a little like a colonialist displaying her loot. It is not that I lack respect for the objects; it is that I have separated them from their religious roots for display purposes.

I justify my ongoing possession of them for teaching purposes, but I still remember the look on one Muslim student's face when he saw me pack a study Qur'an into my book bag under a menorah and a statue of Shiva. I would not have thought twice about doing the same thing with a study Bible, but that was my mistake. A Bible is not a Qur'an, and it was a mistake to assume that a Muslim's attitude toward his holy book was the same as my attitude toward mine.

Let the other define herself, Stendahl cautioned those who engage the faith of others. "Don't think you know the other without listening."[3]

Although my fingers still get a little twitchy when I see a really nice Tibetan temple bell in a shop window, I have learned that possessing an artifact is not the same as possessing the spiritual reality it represents. The jewels of the world's great religions have their own sovereignty. I may look, but I may not poach. As much as I admire the brilliance of the Jewish Talmud—especially the way it hallows sacred debate across the centuries—I cannot have it. It belongs to those in whose lifeblood it was written. As much as my soul leans toward the whirling of the Sufis who bring heaven to earth with their ethereal spinning, I cannot have that either. It belongs to those who have devoted their lives to the love of Allah. This kind of holy envy comes with its own safeguard. Although I am allowed to admire what is growing in the well-tended fields of my religious neighbors, I am not allowed to pull off the road and help myself. The things I envy have their own *terroir*, their own long histories of weather and fertilization. They do not exist to serve me, improve me, or profit me. They have their own dominion.

Another kind of holy envy alerts me to things in other religions that have become neglected in my own, though they may go by different names. Buddhist meditation is not the same as Christian centering prayer, but my envy of the discipline required by the former increases my desire to put more effort into the latter. A Muslim goes to Mecca for different reasons than I go to Bethlehem or Canterbury, but my envy of the Hajj causes me to wonder why I make my pilgrimages alone. What do Muslims know about the power of community that has all but withered from my neglect?

Surely this is what Stendahl meant by his second rule: "Don't compare your best to their worst." Instead, compare your best to their best, so that each becomes better in its own distinct way. Isn't this what the best athletes do? When I see two tennis champions approach the net to shake hands at the end of their match, I like to think that they are not only observing the rules of good sportsmanship but also acknowledging one another's excellence. Later one of them may even watch the match on tape to see what there is to learn from the other. This is how holy envy functions at the top of its game. What I see in the neighbor's yard does not belong to me, but it shows me things in my own yard that I might otherwise have overlooked. If the same thing happens to the neighbors when they look at my yard from their side, we may have a chance to help each other practice our different faiths better.

This brief survey would be incomplete, however, if I did not mention a troubling form of holy envy that keeps me up at night, since it leads me farther from home than I really want to go. This happens when I envy something in another tradition that is so foreign to my own, or so absent from it, that taking it seriously means questioning one of my basic assumptions about how divine reality works. If I want to learn what it has to teach me, I may never see my yard the same way again.

This is what happened when I encountered the Buddhist teaching that human beings are responsible for our own destiny, with no divine mediator to erase our mistakes or offer us a free pass to salvation. Our words and actions have natural consequences, which affect everyone around us. Some lead to joy and some to sorrow, but no one else can handle them for us. They are ours to handle—and to learn from—as best we are able. When the Buddha himself lay dying, his disciples asked him how they could possibly go on without him. Who would guide them after he was gone? "Be lamps unto yourselves," he told them. "Rely on yourselves, and do not rely on external help. Hold fast to the truth as a lamp."[4]

This was so close to something Jesus once said to his disciples—"You are the light of the world" —that I was warmed by the parallel sayings. But I did not find anything in my tradition that came close to the Buddhist view of human ability and responsibility. In the Christian view, human beings are incapable of saving ourselves from our sins. Our only hope is to accept the miraculous intervention of God's only Son, who can take away the consequences of our actions if we let him. In the Episcopal Communion service and in the prayers of the people, we praise Jesus as "our only Mediator and Advocate."

Through long habits of devotion, I learned to love that language along with the restriction and dependence embedded in it, which made the Buddha's dying words all the more startling to me. After I read them, I could not stop thinking about what it might mean to praise Jesus for lighting the fire in me and then to step into the full adulthood of being a lamp unto myself, burning in a community of others who accepted that responsibility with me.

A closely related holy envy flared up when I discovered that neither Judaism nor Islam includes a doctrine of original sin. In the orthodox view of my own tradition, human beings are born with a congenital flaw due to Adam and Eve's original sin in the Garden of Eden. By eating from the one tree God had forbidden them to eat from, the first couple did permanent damage to their offspring, who would all be born with the same tendency to sin. As depressing as this sounds, the doctrine explains why Christians need a Savior who is both fully human (so he has enough in common with us to know what ails us) and fully divine (so he has the power to overcome it).

While different kinds of Christians posit different kinds of remedies—baptism, personal reform, universal reconciliation—

the stain of sin is never entirely eradicated, since it shows up in each generation anew. On days when the entire human race and I seem to be at our worst, this comes as something of a comfort. Sin is in our DNA. At the same time, it drops the bar on being human so low that you have to wonder why we don't all just stay in bed. Weren't Adam and Eve also made in the image of God? What happened to that part of the story?

As I learned from teaching Religion 101, Jews and Muslims also recognize the reality of sin without viewing it as an inherent flaw in human design. In their religious worldviews, God created humans exactly the way we are, with freedom to choose good or evil. God tipped the scales by offering divine guidance in the form of sacred texts and prophets, but no one can do our choosing for us. In this view, Abraham bargains with God on the people's behalf, and Moses pleads their case; Muhammad shows them what perfect submission to God looks like, but God leaves people free to decide how they will respond. No one dooms them to sin, and no one can take their sin away. Humans have everything they need to choose what is good.

Once, after Friday prayer at a masjid, my students and I joined a group of students from other colleges in a circle on the carpet of the prayer hall. The imam who had just led the prayer and delivered the sermon had offered to stay late in order to answer any questions we had. My group was silent, but a young man from another college raised his hand.

"Without Jesus, how do Muslims gain forgiveness from their sins?" he asked.

"Muslims confess their sins directly to God," the imam said, "and God directly forgives them." If we had been in a synagogue instead of a masjid, a rabbi would have said the same thing—an answer that might have given any Christian pause. *Well, that makes sense.* But if it makes sense, then what sense does one make of Jesus's death on the cross?

Holy envy is not a prerequisite for exploring answers to such questions. All one needs is the willingness to enter another religious world and engage those who live there. It helps to be invited and to assume that the people who welcome you are people of goodwill. It also helps if they are skilled at speaking of their faith with people who do not share it, but even under the best of circumstances troubling questions can arise. What is the true nature of God, and how do we know what God desires of us? How capable are we of responding to those desires, and what do we hope will happen to us if we do? If the religious world you are visiting is one where neither "God" nor "religion" is a meaningful term, even more unsettling questions may arise. Is there a larger consciousness at work in what happens to us or are we the makers of our own meaning? What moves people to lives of compassion in the absence of belief in God?

I can think of all sorts of reasons to stay in my own yard. They are often the same reasons students say they do not take religion classes in college: because their elders have warned them to stay away from competing truth claims. Those who leave home anyway are often startled to discover the strenuous benefits of engaging truths different from their own. In the first place, they get to think much more deeply about where their beliefs come from and how well they fit together. In the second place, they get to figure out how to explain their beliefs to people who are not already committed to them. If you are Christian, try explaining the Trinity to someone who does not already believe in it.

In the third place, they get to discover points of contact with neighbors of other faiths along with points of irreconcilable difference. Finally—and this is the most strenuous benefit of all—they get to engage those who are different without feeling compelled to defeat or destroy them. This requires skills. It also requires spiritual and psychological maturity, which makes it a work in progress for humans of any age.

I am not sure whether the virtue of holy envy requires holy humility or creates it, but the two are clearly related. After you have allowed the other to define herself, listening carefully to all the ways in which she is not you, it is hard to overlook the fact that you and she are made of the same basic material. You are dust, and to dust you shall return.

Across all our differences, we come into the world more or less the same way, through the body of another human being. We breathe the same air and depend on the same earth for our sustenance. We all weep salty tears and bleed red blood. Though we find different things funny, we laugh (and sneeze) in amusing ways. Up to a certain age we are so curious about each other that someone has to teach us to fear each other. None of us is born with a belief system or a worldview. We acquire those from our elders, along with our DNA. This does not diminish the importance of our religion, but it does establish a certain priority. What we have most in common is not our religion but our humanity, which is recognizable across class, continent, and color—unless someone goes to great pains to blind us to one another.

Sometimes, on the last day of class, I hand out cards with versions of the Golden Rule on them. "Hurt not others in ways that you yourself would find hurtful." That one is from Judaism. "None of you is a believer until you love for your brother what you love for yourself." That one is from Islam. "This is the sum of duty: do not do to others what would cause pain if done to you." That one is from Hinduism. Some version of the principle shows up in all the great religions of the world, which is a large part of what makes them great: they ask members inside the tribe to use their humanity as the benchmark for how to treat those outside the tribe.

"You shall love your neighbor as yourself." That one is from Christianity. "Do to others as you would have them do to you." That one too.

When students first encounter the reality of multiple religious worldviews, they often race to the lowest common denominator: your truth is true for you and mine is true for me. This is their peace offering, their way of living with religious difference without fighting, but it also prevents them from exploring the differences in any meaningful way. Holy envy gives those students another way forward, especially those who are inclined toward religious absolutes. To embroider a metaphor from the inimitable Robert Farrar Capon, human beings who wish to understand the ways of God are like oysters lying at the bottom of a tide pool, wishing to understand the ways of a prima ballerina.[5] Clearly, there are limits to our abilities. As brilliant as our tide-pool theologies may be, the brilliance of the ballerina exceeds them all. The metaphor is imperfect, to be sure, but it can still free believers to question each other's absolutes, test them, challenge them, and improve them without believing we can know for sure which oyster wins.

This can be difficult for people whose religious histories include a lot of winning. At the moment, Christians and Muslims are tied in that regard, depending on how you measure the rise and fall of empires. Their sacred texts, along with those of Judaism, have lots of strife in them. All three faiths evolved under circumstances in which their followers faced people who wanted to kill them, so they come by their defensiveness honestly. At the same time, all three view God as being the main force behind their victories over their adversaries, who have often included each other. This is old news, but it does complicate the cultivation of holy envy between people who may equate *shared* ground with *lost* ground. It does not help that some of them still want to kill each other—but not all of them, and none of them all the time.

In his book *God and the Universe of Faiths*, British theologian John Hick makes a compelling argument. Before Copernicus, he says, earthlings believed they occupied the center of the universe—and why not? Earth was the place from which they saw everything else. It was the ground under their feet, and as far as they could tell everything revolved around them. Then Copernicus proposed a new map of the universe with the sun at the center and all the planets orbiting around it. His proposal raised religious questions as well as scientific ones, but he was right. The sun, not the earth, holds the planets in our solar system together.

Hick argues that it is past time for a Copernican revolution in theology, in which God assumes the prime place at the center and Christianity joins the orbit of the great religions circling around. Like the scientific revolution, this one requires the surrender of primary place and privileged view. Absolute truth moves to the center of the system, leaving people of good faith with meaningful perceptions of that truth from their own orbits. This new map does not require anyone to give up the claim to uniqueness. It only requires the acceptance of unique neighbors, who concur that the brightness they see at the center of everything exceeds their ability to possess it. The Franciscan father Richard Rohr had his eye on a different planetary body when he said, "We are all of us pointing toward the same moon, and yet we persist in arguing about who has the best finger."[6]

There are dozens of other ways to imagine the relationship of the world's great faiths. Raimon Panikkar, another renowned scholar of religion who was also a Catholic priest, spent a lot of time thinking about what it might mean for Christians to focus on contributing to the world's faiths instead of dominating them. Born in Spain to a Catholic mother and a Hindu father, he used the analogy of the world's great rivers. The Jordan, the Tiber, and the Ganges all nourish the lives of those who live along their banks, he said. One flows through Israel, one flows through Rome, and one flows through India. If he were writing today he might have added the Tigris and Euphrates Rivers, which flow through Turkey, Syria, and Iraq.

None of these rivers meet on earth, Panikkar said, though they do meet in the heavens, where water from each of them condenses into clouds that rain down on all the mortals of the earth. In the same way, he said, the religions of the world remain distinct and unmixed on earth—but "they meet once transformed into vapor, once metamorphosed into Spirit," which then is poured out in innumerable tongues.[7]

Eventually all people of faith must decide how they will think about and respond to people of other (and no) faiths. Otherwise they will be left at the mercy of their worst impulses when push comes to shove and their fear deadens them to the best teachings of their religions.

Once, at the end of a field trip to the Atlanta Masjid of Al-Islam, the imam ended his meeting with students by saying, "Our deepest desire is not that you become Muslim, but that you become the best Christian, the best Jew, the best person you can be. In the name of God, the Most Gracious, the Most Merciful. Thank you for coming." Then he was gone, leaving me with a fresh case of holy envy.

I could do that, I thought. I could speak from the heart of my faith, wishing others well at the heart of theirs—including those who had no name for what got them through the night. It might mean taking down some fences, but turf was no longer the reigning metaphor. I was not imagining two separate yards with neighbors leaning over a shared boundary. I was imagining a single reservoir of living water, with two people looking into it. One might have been a Muslim and the other a Christian, but there was nothing in their faces to tell me that. All I saw were two human beings looking into deep waters that did not belong to either of them, reflecting back to them the truth that they were not alone.

The Nearest Neighbors

This is the kingdom of God, the kingdom of danger
and of risk, of eternal beginning and eternal
becoming, of opened spirit and of deep realization,
the kingdom of holy insecurity.

MARTIN BUBER

My faith in my own tradition took its hardest hit during
the unit on Judaism, for at least two reasons. The first was
that teaching the basics of Jewish belief and practice gave me a
chance to measure how far Christianity had moved from where
it started. By the end of the first century, the religion *of* Jesus had
become the religion *about* him, so that even he might have been
alarmed by what his followers had done. When had the faith of
his ancestors become the adversary? When had people turned
his lifelong faith in the one and only Father to a new faith in the
one and only Son?

This leads directly to the second reason, which was that hearing straight from Jews about Judaism helped me see how much
hatefulness I had absorbed about Jews from Christian scripture
and tradition. Listening to them brought Stendahl's first rule
of religious engagement to mind: "When trying to understand

another religion, you should ask the adherents of that religion
and not its enemies." When I did that—when I let Jews teach me
about Judaism—I found much to envy, though never without a
dose of holy shame for belonging to the religion that had done
theirs so much harm.

When I was in fourth grade my best friend was a dark-haired
girl named Abbie Hoffmann. We attended the same public elementary school in Tuscaloosa, Alabama, where our fathers both
worked at the state university. We lived close enough to walk to
each other's homes, which we did almost every afternoon. One
weekend I went to church with her, riding home with a replica
of Noah's ark made of Popsicle sticks on my lap before the El-
mer's glue had completely dried. Another weekend she invited
me over to see the elaborate hut that her parents had built in
the backyard—a wondrous thing with a slatted roof open to the
sky, where the whole family ate dinner every night for a week
in the fall. I missed Abbie when her family moved to the West
Coast. We quickly lost touch, though when a hippie revolution-
ary named Abbie Hoffman made the news years later, I remembered my fourth-grade friend every time I heard the name.

But how old was I when I realized that Abbie and her family
were Jewish? When did I know that we had gone to a synagogue
instead of a church, and that the hut in her back yard was a suk-
kah built for the Jewish Feast of Tabernacles? How much did I
miss about my best friend because I assumed she was just like
me? And how accustomed was she to being invisible in that way?
These are not questions most ten-year-olds ask, but since I was at
least thirty before I began asking them, there may be something
here worth looking at.

When I ask students in Religion 101 how many of them have
been to a bar or bat mitzvah, two or three raise their hands. A

few more say they have aunts or uncles by marriage who are Jewish. I convince the rest that they know someone who is Jewish by showing them a photo montage of their favorite celebrities: Natalie Portman, Scarlett Johansson, Jake Gyllenhaal, Paul Rudd, Seth Rogan, Jonah Hill, Joseph Gordon-Levitt, Elizabeth Banks, Daniel Radcliffe, Mila Kunis, Shia LaBeouf, and Jon Stewart among many others. Elvis Presley is grandfathered in, since his mother was Jewish. Sometimes I include Marilyn Monroe, who converted to Judaism before marrying the playwright Arthur Miller, and Elizabeth Taylor, whose Jewish name was Elisheba Rachel.

In some ways this opening exercise does more harm than good, since many of these celebrities identify as Jewish without being particularly religious. This is a difficult teaching for Christians—that it is possible to be a secular Jew, who embraces Jewish culture without embracing Jewish religion. When I ask them if they know any Catholics who only attend Mass with their grandmothers, the concept of secular Christians begins to take shape. It is not exactly the same thing, but close enough.

After we parse the differences between Judaism as a religion, a culture, a nation, and a family, the most common question is why Jews do not believe Jesus was the messiah. "Why don't they believe what he said about himself?" one young man asks. "What makes them think Jesus would lie?" His underlying assumption is that all Jews are hostile to Jesus, because that is what he has learned from reading the Bible. It has never occurred to him that there might be good Jewish reasons to decide Jesus was not the Jewish messiah, the same way there might be good Christian reasons to decide that neither Sun Myung Moon nor David Koresh was the Christian messiah.

I hate to tell you that I did not know the difference between

Jewish and Christian concepts of the messiah before teaching Religion 101. Why would I have? I was Christian, with no other frame of reference. The New Testament was my primary source. When I discovered that Jews had their own list of authoritative scriptures about the messiah, I understood that no one was impugning Jesus's character. He simply did not do what Jewish scripture said a messiah would do. He did not restore Jerusalem. He did not rebuild the Jerusalem temple. He did not usher in the age of peace on earth, so that wolves and lambs lay down together and no one learned war anymore. Most Christians expect these things to happen when the Son of God comes *again*, but that is where Jews and Christians part ways. When Jesus's early followers began to worship him, those who confessed faith in the one God waved good-bye to those who saw God as three.

When I arrived at Piedmont, the most visible Jew on campus was a beloved biology professor who looked like a cross between Jerry Garcia and a Hebrew prophet. He took time away from his lab to visit my class more than once, showing us how phylacteries work and teaching us the difference between Ladino and Yiddish, but I knew there was a limit to how often I could ask him to do that. Then for a few years I invited the nearest rabbi to visit, knowing full well it would take him the better part of a day to make the hundred-mile round trip. The first time he came, he blew his shofar for us, saying he was pretty sure he was the first Jew ever to do that in Habersham County.

Then one day a young man who wishes to be called Shlomo showed up in class wearing a fedora. He was Jewish on his mother's side. He had studied for several years at a yeshiva in Jerusalem. He had returned home to live with his father's Christian parents in a neighboring county, which was how he ended up at Piedmont College. This was interesting in all sorts of ways, not least of which was that Shlomo identified as an Orthodox Jew. He quickly eclipsed the biology professor as the MVJ (Most Visible Jew) on campus and seemed to enjoy the role.

I know I did. Shlomo had the entire Talmud on his cell phone. He could give me an educated answer to any question I asked him about a fine point of Jewish law. While I had to suppress the urge to make him the spokesman for worldwide Jewry in Religion 101, he was happy to share his experience of being an observant Jew with students both in and out of class. When we got to the unit on Judaism, all he had to do was be there to bring the material to life.

Shlomo helped me zero in on things I envied about Judaism. There was first of all his intentional observance of the Sabbath, which, like his understanding of the messiah, was based on scripture. I was used to seeing Christians riding lawnmowers on the Sabbath, trimming tight circles around the Ten Commandment signs in their yards, but Shlomo cut no corners. He did not work on the Sabbath. He did not cause anyone else to work on the Sabbath either. He rested on the seventh day—as God did, scripture says, and as God commanded humans to do—sanctifying rest as the natural, regular, and holy fulfillment of work.

Once, when Shlomo volunteered to welcome guests at a Saturday religion conference, I tried to pay him for his time. He reminded me that he could not accept money on the Sabbath. I bought him a Barnes & Noble gift card instead, which he returned because he said it was the same thing. Finally I gave up and accepted his presence as a free gift. Later, when he lowered his standards to go on a field trip to a Reform temple in Atlanta, on a Friday night (Orthodox Jews do not ride in cars on the Sabbath), he was the only student who showed up in a suit and tie.

After the service we went to a Middle Eastern restaurant where I knew Shlomo could get kosher food, but I had not given a single thought to the belly dancing that was a regular feature on Friday nights. When the women came out just before the dessert course with glitter glued to their bare midriffs, Shlomo quietly excused himself and waited patiently in the parking lot while the rest of us finished our baklava. Years later, when I offered him a stipend for reviewing this chapter of *Holy Envy*, he refused, insisting it was a *mitzvah* (a good deed done to honor God). Shlomo is a *mensch*.

This marginality of his was something else I envied. Because he belonged to a religious minority—and practiced his religion in a way that made him unusual even among other practicing Jews—he was intentional about his faith in a way that stood out. Everything from his fedora to his Sabbath practice reminded me that the root word for "holy" in Hebrew is *kadosh*, meaning set apart for special purpose, as ordinary food is set apart by saying a blessing over it, or as a person is set apart by taking special vows to become married or ordained. I saw other people in Habersham County whose religious identity set them apart, such as the Old German Baptist couple at the grocery store who wore plain dress like the Amish or the Buddhist monk with his shaved head and orange robes. Although I was not sure I wanted people looking at me the same way I looked at them, I did wonder what it would feel like to get dressed in the morning knowing that my faith would make me odd.

My faith is invisible to most people, especially since I stopped wearing a clergy collar, though everything from the school holiday calendar to the greeting-card section at the drugstore supports my sense of being in the religious mainstream. I do not have to look for a kosher cut of meat when I have company over for dinner or decline dinner invitations to households that mix meat and dairy. Of course a Buddhist monk has his own challenges when mealtime rolls around, but Christians think of Jews as very close kin. We share so much heritage that we often speak of "the Judeo-Christian tradition" as if it were one instead of two. Shlomo reminded me how many differences that hyphen really spans. A plus/minus symbol might work better, since the things that separate us are as vital to our identities as the things that we have in common.

At the same time, Shlomo lived with Christians he loved, which gave him the ability to speak across the hyphen. He had ready answers for the evangelists who pursued him, delivering up counter-arguments that were biblically sound and theologically shrewd, fully meant to extend the dialog instead of end it. This was difficult for some of his classmates not only because they were unused to being challenged by someone who had thought things through so clearly, but also because Shlomo was coming from a whole different place. He did not share their assumptions about scripture, the messiah, or God's plan for salvation. Works were good for him, not bad. God's law was a treasure, not a burden. Righteousness was a response to God's grace, not a substitute for it.

I had been a pastor for at least ten years when a letter from California arrived in my mailbox at church. It came from a Jewish psychiatrist who said that he had been reading some of my published sermons. While he found much to appreciate in them, he said, he was sorry to note that I was still using the "language of contempt." I could not imagine what he meant, which was the beginning of our correspondence. With kindness and clarity, he showed me how I used stock phrases such as "the burden of the law" or "the righteousness of the Pharisees" to make my points without the slightest idea how they sounded to Jewish ears. He helped me see how I perpetuated the Gospels' portrayal of "the Jews" without drawing attention to the imprecision of the phrase or the reasons why it was used so venomously. In short, he showed me how casually I appropriated the language of the New Testament without thinking about how the past twenty centuries affect its hearing today.

He was right. I had lived so long in the mainstream that I never even thought about how I sounded from the margins. My audiences were exclusively Christian. I spoke to them in Christian language, which was loaded with exclusivity. So much of the New Testament was written by people at odds with the Judaism of their time that their anti-Judaism was baked into the gospel. If I spoke the language of contempt with ease, it was because that language was so embedded in the Christian narrative that I did not even hear it when it reared up and hissed.

That it took Jews to wake me up to this is important. Our shadows are often behind us, where others can see them better than we can. If we want to hear and see more—even the parts that expose our scornfulness—we need partners from outside our in-groups to keep telling us how we sound. Some of them get tired of doing this, I know, since those of us in the mainstream are not particularly fast learners. The people who stick with us seem to understand that they can benefit as much as we do, since one of the best ways to learn more about your faith is to engage people who do not share it. The more we mix it up with others, the more we find out about who we really are.

Jews have had a lot more practice with this than most Christians have. Part of it is numerical, since Judaism is the smallest of the world's great religions. This multiplies the odds of encountering people who do not share your faith. But another part of it is theological, since Judaism has always recognized that God made more than one covenant with humankind. God's exclusive covenant with Jews exists inside God's inclusive covenant with all people.

This is one of the things I envy most about Judaism. When I first learned about the Jewish custom of actively discouraging converts, I assumed it was a "no room at the inn" kind of response. "So sorry you didn't call sooner, but the covenant with God is all filled up." As it turned out, this was not the case at all. Depending on which rabbi you ask, sending potential converts away three times is meant to remind them that there is nothing easy about being Jewish. Having to pester an uncooperative rabbi may be the smallest obstacle a convert ever faces. But the more important teaching is that a person does not have to be Jewish to be righteous in God's eyes. According to Jewish tradition, God made a covenant with Noah that included all people before making a covenant with Abraham that included one particular people. Between the two covenants God has everyone covered, and the one does not replace the other.

In the words of Jonathan Sacks, who served for twenty-two years as Chief Rabbi of the United Hebrew Congregations of the Commonwealth:

The God of Israel is larger than the specific practices of Israel. Traces of his presence can be found throughout the world. We do not have to share a creed or code to be partners in the covenant of mankind. The prophets of Israel wrestle with an idea still counterintuitive to the Platonic mind: that moral and spiritual dignity extend far beyond the boundaries of any one civilization. They belong to the

other, the outsider, the stranger, the one who does not fit
our system, race, or creed.[1]

I was awash with holy envy when I read that. Why didn't my
faith have a teaching like that? Why was my religion so set on being the sun? Judaism sees the universe differently, and it makes a
difference in how Jews welcome religious strangers.

Once, when I took a bunch of students to a Saturday morning
Shabbat service in Atlanta, we thought we had gotten the time
wrong since there were so few other people there. The Temple
administrator had told me there were no bar or bat mitzvahs
scheduled for that morning—which was a shame, since witness-
ing that ceremony teaches students more about Judaism than
the chapter in their textbook—but the day worked on the class
schedule, so we went.

The Temple is an Atlanta landmark, not only because of its
age and beauty, but also because of the congregation's activism
during the American civil rights movement. In October 1958,
a group of white supremacists retaliated by placing fifty sticks
of dynamite at the north entrance to the Temple, blowing that
corner of the building apart. Originally founded as the Hebrew
Benevolent Congregation in 1867, the Temple's benevolence
continues today, touching lives across the Southeast through its
commitment to social justice and religious tolerance.

The main sanctuary holds more than a thousand people on
high holy days, so on the morning of the field trip it was easy
to see that there were only eighteen people there and eleven of
them were us. The rabbi took this in as she entered the room to
welcome the congregation. Since she knew we were coming, she
introduced us to the other people who were there as well as to
the cantor (who was also a woman) before making sure we all

had prayer books and were on the right page. Then the cantor began the morning service, and we were off to the races—some of us trying to sing along with her in Hebrew and others taking in the splendor of the space without trying to keep up at all. When the time came for the reading of the Torah, the rabbi looked at us and said, "Do you want to come up here and stand around me while I read?" This would not have happened at any church I knew of, so I was not prepared. The students looked at me for a clue as to what they should do.

"You don't have to go," I said, "but I'm going."

Every single student stood up to follow me. The cantor waited until we had all shuffled out of our pew and arrived at the lectern, where she arranged us around the rabbi so we could all see the Torah scroll in front of her. Then the cantor picked up the *yad*—a golden pointer shaped like an arm with an extended index finger at the end—and aimed it at a line of Hebrew text so the rabbi knew where to begin. When I leaned in, I felt the softness of the rabbi's prayer shawl against my arm. Her body swelled every time she took a breath to read the next line. The Hebrew words came out of her mouth like a murmuration of birds she had released from the page. The students held very still around me, as stupefied as I was to be standing where we stood. When I looked up at the members of the congregation, they were smiling at us like grandparents.

As often as I have worried about how a class visit might disrupt other people's worship, my hosts of other faiths have never yet shared my concern. Over and over, they seem glad that students want to know more about a religious tradition whose followers are in the low single digits of the US population.

On another class visit—this time to a new Sephardic congregation in the suburbs that met in the basement of a Methodist church—the students and I discovered that we had arrived on Simchat Torah, the day when the annual cycle of public Torah readings ends and a new one begins. Among many other things, this meant that at a certain point in the service the two rabbis (a man and a woman who were married to each other) invited the whole congregation to rise and dance behind them as they carried a huge Torah scroll around the room.

"Yes, you too," the woman rabbi said when she saw my eyebrows go up. So the students and I rose and joined the dance line, adding all our best moves to the others on display, while the members of the congregation sang loud happy songs with lots of "Heys!" in them. When the Torah scroll had made it all the way around the room seven times and the last song had come to an end, we all went back to our folding chairs and sat there panting while the rabbis put the scroll back where it belonged, adjusted their kippahs and prayer shawls, and got ready for the next part of the service.

When the woman rabbi stepped up to the microphone, she said, "You know, sometimes those of us who are here every week get so used to things that we forget how important they are. Then one week we welcome some visitors for the first time, and they enter in with more enthusiasm than we do. It's a good reminder, isn't it?" *Holy envy, from the Jewish point of view.* She turned to where the students and I were sitting, looked down the whole row of us, and said, "You Gentiles sure can dance!"

I have many memories like this one, in which I felt warmly included by a tradition other than my own, but most of the students have never visited a synagogue before and may never visit one again. That makes it hard to decide where to take them on their one and only field trip. If I take them to a synagogue where the cantor and rabbi are both women, they will come away with an entirely different view of Judaism than if I take them to one where men and women sit in different sections. If I take them to a landmark like the Temple, they will think of Judaism differently than if I take them to a service in the basement of a church. Wherever we end up going, there is no way to control how students will interpret what they see or hear or what they will tell other people they saw and heard when they return home.

In the van on the way home from the Temple I eavesdrop on a student talking on her cell phone. She is telling her mother about the visit, delivering her conclusions about Jewish faith and practice based on her recent firsthand experience. *Wait!* I want to shout. *You've only been to one place!* She sounds like a traveler who has eaten a single meal at a single airport restaurant during a two-hour layover at JFK, which has become her gold standard for the character of the American people and their food.

As alarming as it is to think about the impact that a single visit can have, there is a truth here that I do not want to miss: it is not what we believe that defines us, but what we do.

When visitors come to a worship service in my own religious tradition, a great deal depends on how warmly they are welcomed and whether they feel included or excluded by what they hear during the short time they are with us. We may have exactly one shot at communicating who we are to people who know nothing about us—or who think they already know a lot about us—but who, in either case, will remember us as the embodiment of our entire tradition, the prime exemplars of our faith.

In her book *Out of Africa*, the Danish author Karen Blixen (writing under the pen name Isak Dinesen) tells the story of a young Kikuyu boy named Kitau who appeared at her door in Nairobi one day to ask if he might work for her. She hired him on the spot. Kitau served her household so admirably that she was stricken when, after just three months, he asked for a letter of recommendation to a Muslim in Mombasa named Sheik Ali. Since Blixen did not want to lose Kitau, she offered to increase his pay, but he was firm in his desire to leave.

He had decided that he was going to become either a Christian or a Muslim, he explained to her. His whole purpose in coming to live with her had been to see the ways and habits of Christians up close. Next he would go to live with Sheik Ali for three months to see how Muslims behaved. Then he would make up his mind. Aghast, Blixen wrote, "I believe that even an Archbishop, when he had had these facts laid before him, would have said, or at least thought, as I said, 'Good God, Kitau, you might have told me that when you came here!'"

The fact that Kitau was weighing the habits of Christians and not their beliefs is relevant, since on the whole Jews are less interested in beliefs than Christians are. Jewish identity hinges on how one lives, not what one thinks—another source of holy envy for me. Sometimes, when I am eavesdropping on students in the college van, I am sobered by the questions they ask each other to determine how Christian they are:

"Do you believe in the virgin birth and the physical resurrection?"

"Do you believe the Bible is the inerrant word of God?"

"Do you believe Jesus is the only way to God?"

Few of them know that the items on their orthodoxy checklist do not date from the first century but from the early twentieth, when the Bible Institute of Los Angeles published a series of essays to establish the fundamentals of Christian belief.[2] I wish the Institute had spent as much time on the fundamentals of Christian practice, so that students had more to talk about than what they believe. After all these years behind the wheel of the college van, I am still waiting to hear a single student vet another's faith by asking a different set of questions:

"How does being Christian change the way you live?"

"What's the hardest part about loving your neighbor as yourself?"

"What is your favorite way to pray?"

"Well done is better than well said," reads a country church sign near my house. It is a teaching that Jews and Christians have in common, though Christians often need reminding that our beliefs are just things we say unless they lead to things we actually do. A Jew might not put it that way, but it is another central teaching that inspires holy envy in me.

When I first started looking for the Jewish equivalent to the Nicene Creed (one of the earliest statements of Christian belief), I learned that there is no mandatory set of beliefs for Jews. A famous twelfth-century rabbi named Maimonides came up with thirteen principles of Jewish faith, but there is nothing binding about them. What is binding, for Jews who choose to be bound, is Jewish practice: how to worship; how to pray; how to conduct business; how to care for the land; how to treat the neighbor, the stranger, the widow, and the orphan. It is all about relationships. The closest thing I could find to a Jewish creed was the Shema, a combination of three biblical passages that begins with Deuteronomy 6:4: "Hear, O Israel! The LORD is our God, the LORD alone" (JPS).

As small as the first word of that verse is, it made a big impression on me. What must it be like, I wondered, to put *hearing* God ahead of being heard? So many of the prayers in my own tradition are about beseeching God to hear us. So much of our worship involves listening to each other talk and then going out to proclaim the gospel to others. What do we think will happen if we stop talking? The Jewish emphasis on hearing and doing are both curative for me. "Hear, O Barbara! The LORD is your God, even when you are mute."

The day I bring kosher food to class clarifies the relationship between belief and practice. There are so many grocery bags in my car that I have to arrive thirty minutes early and make two trips, so that when the students arrive they will find mountains of foodstuffs piled on the tables before them: Pringles, Pop-Tarts, Reese's peanut butter cups, Cracker Jacks, Jello-cup snacks, Starkist tuna lunch kits, Vienna sausages, party-sized packages of Lay's potato chips, tubs of Betty Crocker chocolate frosting, Lindt Lindor truffles, and Blue Diamond smoked almonds. When students come through the door and see all of this, their faces light up as if they have just arrived at the heavenly banquet. The rule is that they may eat anything with a kosher symbol on it. Then they have to tell me why the other things are not kosher.

This exercise takes over class as fast as the singing bowls did. Students race to tell the difference between a trademark symbol, a copyright symbol, and a kosher symbol. When they agree they have found one of the kosher symbols from the list I have supplied, there is a shout of triumph as they rip open bags of Reese's or pop the tops on cans of Pringles. With their mouths full, they bend over a tin of Spam trying to figure out what is wrong with it. I could tell them all kinds of things that are wrong with it, but they focus on the pork. "Two kinds!" one of them says, pointing to the ingredient label. "Pork shoulder *and* ham!"

As elementary as this exercise is, it does one vital thing that can never be undone: it convinces students that Judaism has been right there in front of them all along, only they could not see it because they were not looking. Now some of them will never pick up a bag of sour cream–flavored potato chips again without showing a friend the little *D* (for dairy) inside the certified kosher triangle on the label.

Some will take the exercise a step further by trying to keep modified kosher food laws for a day, which is an option on their list of elective assignments. For twenty-four hours they agree to avoid shellfish, pork, and pork by-products; to separate meat from dairy by at least three hours; and to make sure that all the snack foods they eat have kosher symbols on them. One student reports that his first crisis came at breakfast, when he realized he could not have his usual bowl of cheese grits and bacon topped with Lucky Charms. Another student reports that the bacon on her salad was already on its way down before she realized that it was, in fact, pork. By the end of the day some are so worn out from thinking about food that they skip dinner and go straight to bed, while others express fresh appreciation for being Christian, since it means they can eat anything they want.

"I honestly was not expecting to learn anything from this assignment," one student wrote. "I just thought it looked easy. Who knew food could teach you life lessons? Saying you love God is one thing; changing the way you eat for God is something else altogether." She was not Jewish, she said, but she had borrowed Jewish shoes, and she would remember the feel of them for years to come.

Every now and then I meet a student who had little exposure to religious teaching growing up. This is hard to believe in the deep South, but also refreshing, since those students seem not to have sucked up as much invective as their more religious peers. Rochel was one of those. When she became a spiritual seeker in high school, she did it with an almost blank slate. "People made fun of my Jewfro," she said (a variation on "Afro"), so she figured that was a good place to start. When a rabbi heard her tell her story at a Jewish summer camp, he heard something that convinced him to bypass the traditional wisdom about sending her away three times. He came up to her afterward and offered to sponsor her conversion, which was already under way when she signed up for Religion 101.

Rochel was a great student, full of questions and unafraid to speak up in class. During the unit on Judaism, when I tried to honor her extracurricular learning by asking her a question about minor prophets or lesser holidays, she would cheerfully say, "I haven't gotten that far yet." But as soon as she saw the list of elective assignments for the class, she asked if she could do an oral report on welcoming the Sabbath.

"Yes," I said. "Please. That would be wonderful."

When the day came, she took over my desk up front, pulling one thing after another out of her overstuffed backpack. First she shook a white cloth in the air and covered the table with it. Then she dug out a candle, a plate, and a cup.

"You'll have to imagine the challah and the wine," she said to her classmates when everything was ready. "Also another candle, since there are supposed to be two." Then she settled her prayer shawl over her shoulders, lit the candle, and waved her hands over its flame, pulling the light toward her face in a gesture as old as time. The only sound in the room was people breathing. When she began the Hebrew blessing over the imaginary bread, using the ancient melody her rabbi had taught her, the walls of the classroom fell away. Her song took us someplace most of us had never been. When she stumbled in her new language, she quickly recovered and let the song lead her on.

This was not a performance. This was a prayer. By the time

she said the blessing over the imaginary wine, it was clear there was nothing imaginary about her devotion. Rochel became a Jew the following year by full immersion in a community *mikvah*. Last Passover she invited all of her Gentile friends over for supper. She is still working on her Hebrew.

Will she remain a Jew forever? Is she in the vanguard of a generation who will choose a faith with no help from their elders? The scary beauty of the present time is that no one has reliable answers to such questions. What we have instead are the great religions of the world, all pointing at something beyond themselves, and these fragile souls of ours, tilted toward the divine mystery that enfolds all our lives.

Disowning God

God speaks to us in three places: in scripture, in our deepest selves, and in the voice of the stranger.

THOMAS MERTON

When I was not teaching at Piedmont, I was traveling around the country speaking at university chapels, churches, and continuing-education events. The contrast between the classroom and the stage was dramatic. The classroom was my kitchen, where I cooked up something different for the students every week. I wore comfortable shoes that let me dash from the lectern to the white board to the computer on the podium, scattering colored markers as I went. Sometimes I only made it halfway through my class plan, because a student pressed a question that was more interesting than the plan. I even knew what the quiet ones were thinking, since I read their papers late into the night.

Things were quite different on the road. When I packed for the airport, my best suits went into the suitcase along with a carefully prepared manuscript and a pair of heels I knew would torture me every step of the way. They were my hair shirt, meant to remind me that I had left the kitchen for the banquet hall. In short order I would be standing in front of hundreds of people who rightfully expected me to say something both intelligent and complete. They had read things I had written but I had read nothing of theirs, which made this job the opposite of the classroom. There would be no home cooking in front of the microphone. The dish I served had to be innovative, delectable, and beautifully presented.

There was still great synergy between the two kinds of work. What happened in the classroom informed my talks on the stage, where I was often called upon to speak to Christians who were engaged in their own religious reformations. The majority of them were my age or older. White hair was the norm. They had taken or taught every course their churches had to offer and were still hungry for more. The faith that had sustained them through their middle years had gotten as tight as their old clothes. Their views of God, scripture, the church, and the world were all under renovation.

In many ways, they reminded me of college students. They were eager. They were ready to think in new ways about important things. They took notes while I talked. What made them different was their long immersion in Christian faith, practice, and imagination. When I made fast turns, they kept up with me. There was no need to stop and define my terms. Because they were biblically literate and fluent in the Christian language, it was possible to explore things with them that it was neither possible nor appropriate to explore with college students. For all these reasons and more, I began to approach the stage as a place to deal with the personal questions that were coming up for me in the classroom.

What does it mean to be a person of faith in a world of many faiths?

If God is revealed in many ways, why follow the
Christian way?

Is Christian faith primarily about being Christian or
becoming truly human?

How does loving Jesus equip me to love those who do not
love him the way I do?

What do religious strangers reveal to me about God?

Just as questions like these were gaining urgency for me, I
received an invitation to give a baccalaureate address at a small
university in upstate New York. The chaplain went over the details in her letter. The student body was religiously diverse, she
said. If I accepted, I would share the stage with leaders of Jewish
and Muslim student organizations. The audience would also include Asian students and their families from a variety of traditions along with some who claimed no religious affiliation. "We
hope you will speak from your own religious tradition while
avoiding exclusive or triumphal language," she wrote.

I had to stop and think about that sentence, because no one
had ever said anything like that to me before. My audiences on
the road had been uniformly Christian, with some diversity
among the mainline Protestants in the room, but no obvious
differences in race, culture, or country of origin. So that was one
thing. The other thing was the "exclusive or triumphal language"
part, which reminded me of what I had learned from the Jewish
psychiatrist about the unconscious language of contempt. I did
not think I sounded exclusive or triumphal, but wouldn't I be the
last to know?

I accepted the invitation with no idea how much it would

change me. If the apostle Paul's conversion made scales fall from his eyes, mine made plugs fall from my ears. When I attended church services, I heard things come out of my mouth that I had not really listened to for years. These included some all-time favorite hymns, such as the thrilling one that begins, "Crown him with many crowns, the Lamb upon his throne; / Hark! how the heavenly anthem drowns all music but its own."[1] I have sung that hymn many times with gusto, without giving a thought to those whose music I might be drowning out.

Another favorite hymn mourns Israel's lonely exile from the Son of God. Another yearns for a future in which every knee will bow to Jesus. Another urges Christian soldiers onward, marching as to war. When I imagined singing it with a Muslim or Hindu student sitting next to me, my voice dried up. It was a song for insiders, not outsiders. If I had learned anything from going on all of those class field trips, it was how religious language sounds to outsiders, and how much that matters.

After I started hearing the hymns differently, scripture was next. This was not an entirely new exercise for me, since I was once an outsider to Christianity myself. I knew how scripture sounded from the perspective of the damned, but the memory had dimmed. I had not stayed outside Christianity, after all. I had made my way in, where I had acquired the skills to read the Bible in much greater depth, with far more nuance. Once the plugs fell from my ears, however, I was reminded how scripture might still sound to someone who heard it with no padding.

The language of contempt is not the only shadow language in the New Testament. There is also one that uses the rhetoric of men first, followed by silenced women and obedient slaves. There is another that divides reality into opposed pairs, pitting church against world, spirit against flesh, light against dark. There is even one that glorifies suffering for suffering's sake, leading some Christians to hurt themselves—or others—for reasons that have nothing to do with the gospel.

The purpose of staying on the lookout for languages like these is to prevent them from becoming uncontested parts of the Christian worldview. Every time I run into one of them hard enough to hurt, I turn around and look in the opposite direction, where there is almost always a counternarrative in scripture just waiting for someone to notice it. When I run into a hard corner of Christian thinking about the subordination of women, I remember that the angel Gabriel did not ask Mary's father if it would be all right for her to bear a son out of wedlock; Gabriel asked *her*. When I am walloped by Christian condescension toward those who are not Christian, I remember how many religious strangers played lead roles in Jesus's life: the Canaanite woman who expanded his sense of agency, the Samaritan leper who showed him what true gratitude looked like, the Roman centurion in whom he saw more faith than he had ever seen in one of his own tribe.

If narratives like these are easy to overlook—or worse yet, to distort—then that is because our accustomed ways of hearing scripture often stop our ears to what is actually on the page. The old tape starts playing and we just let it run. This is one of the reasons why I remain a devoted student of the Bible: because what it says is so often *not* what I have been taught it says, or what I think it says, or what I want it to say. Scripture has its own voice— sometimes more terrible than wonderful—but it has never failed to reward my close attention, either with a fresh hearing or with the loud slamming of a door that tells me to come back later.

Why persist? Because in a world where empires rise and fall, where legendary places of worship become museums, and where operating systems of all kinds have shorter and shorter life spans, the Bible offers me ballast that little else can. I turn to it the same way chemists turn to the periodic table or Supreme Court judges turn to the Constitution. It is my baseline in matters of faith—something far older than I am, with a great deal more experience in what it means to be both human and divine. There are times when I read the Bible literally—as when Moses complains about what a royal pain in the ass it is to be a religious leader, or when Jesus nails an inquisitor on his or her own iniquity—but on the whole I read it literarily, as the consummate work of divinely inspired human memory and imagination that I believe it is.

When religious arguments based on the perspective of a single century or culture reach a high pitch, or when people who seem to have read only excerpts of the Bible use it to propose legislation, I return to the Book—not to find a solution, but to remember how many possibilities there are. There are passages that make me want to take a pair of scissors to them and others that I have copied in calligraphy for framing, but that seems to be the point. The Bible is bigger than I am. It does not care what I like and do not like. It preceded me by millennia and will likely still be around when my civilization returns to dust.

In the meantime, the Bible not only connects me to people around the world who hear it in different languages and whose experience leads them to interpret it in different ways; it also gives me a place to meet people right here at home who are equally devoted to it, though for different reasons and to different ends. Every time someone wants to argue about what God or Jesus or Paul *really* said, I say, "Show me where."

Once, in a class on the book of Genesis, a student challenged me after I noted one of Abraham's more regrettable character flaws, which was to pass his wife Sarah off as his sister so that other men could have her without thinking they had to kill him first.

"But she *was* his sister," the student said, somewhat missing the point.

"Show me where," I said, not believing her for a minute. The next time class met, she had her Bible with her, and she *did* show me where. In Genesis 20:12, Abraham says that his wife Sarah is also his half sister—the daughter of his father by a different mother. You could have knocked me over with a feather. The student won the scripture duel fair and square. She enjoyed winning, and I enjoyed finding a verse that had been hidden in plain sight. I hope she is still telling the story, just as I am, though it may only be of interest to people who spend as much time studying a twenty-five-hundred-year-old book as other people spend playing games on their phones.

The problem with every sacred text is that it has human readers. Consciously or unconsciously, we interpret it to meet our own needs. There is nothing wrong with this unless we deny that we are doing it, as when someone tells me that he is not "interpreting" anything but simply reporting what is right there on the page. This is worrisome, not only because he is reading a translation from the original Hebrew or Greek that has already involved a great deal of interpretation, but also because it is such a short distance between believing you possess an error-free message from God and believing that you are an error-free messenger of God. The literalists I like least are the ones who do not own a Bible. The literalists I like most are the ones who admit that they do not understand every word God has revealed in the Bible, though they still believe God has revealed it. I can respect that.

I can respect almost anyone who admits to being human while reading a divine text. After that, we can talk—about why we highlight some teachings and ignore others, about how we decide which ones are historically conditioned and which ones are universally true, about who has influenced our reading of scripture and how our social location affects what we hear. The minute I believe I know the mind of God is the minute someone needs to sit me down and tell me to breathe into a paper bag.

Once my holy envy led me to ask more of my tradition than the narrative of exclusive salvation and everlasting triumph, I began to search for counternarratives that sounded more like Jesus to me. In particular, I looked for stories that supported Christian engagement with religious strangers—not as potential converts but as agents of the God who transcends religion and never *met* a stranger. Beginning with the Persian magi in Matthew's Gospel and ending with the Roman centurion who recognizes Jesus as the Son of God, the Gospels are full of such characters—people who come from beyond the tribe to bless the tribe and then return to where they came from. In Judaism they are called "righteous gentiles." I do not know what they are called in Christianity, but Jesus receives them more than once, whether they come from Samaria, Syrophoenicia, Canaan, or Rome. In story after story, they enter stage left, deliver their blessing on the Christian gospel, and exit stage right, leaving their mark on a tradition that is not their own.

If it is easy for Christians to overlook the "otherness" of these religious strangers, then I think that is because we assume that once they enter our story they never leave it. In gratitude for their blessing, we baptize them as anonymous Christians. We make them one of us. A few do join us, but this is not the norm. In the case of the Persian magi, their appearance in Bethlehem is as surprising as a delegation of Methodist bishops arriving in Dharamsala to recognize the next incarnation of the Dalai Lama. Once they deliver their gifts to the starlit Hebrew baby, they go back to where they came from, presumably to resume their vocations as Zoroastrian priests. Yet every Christmas we sing of them in church, as if they had never left.

This tradition of strangers bearing divine gifts begins early in the Bible with the story of Melchizedek, a Canaanite king and priest who comes out of nowhere bearing bread and wine for Abraham (then Abram) after a great battle. You can find it in Genesis 14 if you want, but since it is only four verses long you are also welcome to my summary.

First Melchizedek blesses Abram in the name of the God Most High, whom he serves. At no point is there any discussion about whether Melchizedek's God and Abram's God are the same God. After blessing Abram, Melchizedek blesses God. In gratitude, Abram gives him a tenth of everything. Then Melchizedek exits the story as suddenly as he entered it, leaving Abram to become Abraham, the father of the Jews. The End.

Though Jews and Christians have made much of this mysterious stranger, some going as far as offering up elaborate interpretations of Melchizedek's identity in order to establish their own priority, the story needs no embellishment. As short as it is, the narrative already has a clear message in place: God works through religious strangers. For reasons that will never be entirely clear, God sometimes sends people from outside a faith community to bless those inside of it. It does not seem to matter if the main characters understand God in the same way or call God by the same name. The divine blessing is effective, and the story goes on.

Other examples of redemptive religious strangers in the first testament of the Bible include Bithiah, the Pharaoh's daughter who plucked the baby Moses from his rush basket in the River Nile and raised him as her own; Jethro, the Midianite priest who was Moses's father-in-law and teacher; Ruth, the Moabite who became the ancestor of King David; and Cyrus, the Persian king who ended the Babylonian exile and allowed the Jews to return home—the only non-Jew in the Bible who is ever identified as God's anointed one.[2]

Perhaps stories like these help explain why the divine command to love the stranger shows up so often in Jewish teaching. It appears for the first time in Exodus as the direct word of God. "You shall not wrong a stranger or oppress him" (22:20, JPS), God says in the same speech that includes the Ten Commandments. In subsequent speeches, God presses the point home.

> "When a stranger resides with you in your land, you shall
> not wrong him. The stranger who resides with you
> shall be to you as one of your citizens; you shall love
> him as yourself, for you were strangers in the land of
> Egypt: I the LORD am your God." (Lev. 19:33–34, JPS)

> "When you reap the harvest in your field and overlook
> a sheaf in the field, do not turn back to get it; it shall
> go to the stranger, the fatherless, and the widow—in
> order that the LORD your God may bless you in all your
> undertakings." (Deut. 24:19, JPS)

> "You and the stranger shall be alike before the LORD."
> (Num. 15:15b, JPS)

However you define the problematic present-day stranger— the religious stranger, the cultural stranger, the transgendered stranger, the homeless stranger—scripture's wildly impractical solution is to love the stranger as the self. You are to offer the stranger food and clothing, to guarantee the stranger justice, to treat the stranger like one of your own citizens, to welcome the stranger as Christ in disguise. This is God's express will in both testaments of the Bible.

Once, walking down a street full of food trucks in Portland, Oregon, I passed a young man working on a new sign to hold up to passers-by. He was so smartly dressed that I wondered if he were there by choice instead of necessity. He also had very good penmanship. When I saw what he was writing on his sign, I was glad to be getting past him before he held it up. "What if I am an angel," his sign read, "and this is a test?" *What a clever young man*, I thought.

The remarkable thing about the stranger-loving commands in the Bible is that they appear in the sacred scriptures of Jews and Christians, which are honored by Muslims as well. By all rights, you would expect such scriptures to protect a religious community's privileges and diminish the rights of those who do not belong to it, but that is not the case. Instead, these communities have chosen to preserve commands that clarify God's care for outsiders as well as insiders, religious strangers as well as friends.

There is no story in the New Testament that conveys this better than the story of Jesus's first sermon in his home synagogue at Nazareth. Only Luke tells it. Jesus has just emerged from forty days in the wilderness, where he was sorely tested by self-interest. The devil had suggested all kinds of ways that Jesus could take magnificent care of himself—by turning a stone into a loaf of bread to end his hunger, by becoming king of the world to secure his power, by summoning angels to protect him from all harm. All Jesus had to do was ask, the devil said, and God would make sure that he did not so much as stub a toe.

Jesus resisted all of these blandishments, emerging from the wilderness as weak and lean as a man ever was. His emptiness left plenty of room for the Spirit to fill him up, which it did. Jesus used the strength the Spirit gave him to make his way back home—from the desert in the south, where John the Baptist had baptized him, to his hometown of Nazareth in the north, where his mother, Mary, still lived. If the Bible were a documentary instead of a book, the narrator would speak over a map of all the places Jesus stopped on his way back home, with each place lighting up as he passed through. He taught in synagogues along the way, Luke says, and everyone who heard him was full of praise. When he finally reached the region of Galilee where he had grown up, his reputation had preceded him. It was only a matter of time before he taught in his hometown synagogue, where expectations would be running very high.

"When he came to Nazareth, where he had been brought up," Luke says, "he went to the synagogue on the sabbath day, as was his custom." Jesus was an observant Jew, in other words, but even if he had not been, he would probably have gone to the synagogue on his first weekend back home. Once, when I asked an active churchman why there were so many more men in church on Christmas and Easter than on ordinary Sundays, he said, "Insistent wives and mothers?"

When it came time for the appointed scripture to be read, someone handed the scroll of the prophet Isaiah to Jesus. Was he self-conscious? Any other favorite son would have been. Some of the people sitting in front of him were sure to remark on how his voice had changed, while others would note the places where his pronunciation could have been better. Some would not have been listening at all, trying to find the image of the boy they once knew in the face of the man he had become.

A few would wonder why he had never married. A few more would slide their eyes over to Mary, watching her watch her boy do his thing.

He was their boy too after all. Plenty of them had kept an eye on him when he was little and Mary was busy with the wash basket or the water bucket. When he had needed scolding they knew they had her permission to do it, and when he had needed comforting they did that too. Even those who had not particularly liked children would have felt possessive of him, now that he had become a famous man. Whatever their relationship to him, they had heard about the things he did on his way back home to them—the surprising sermons, the supernatural healings. They could not wait to find out what he had saved up for them. If Jesus's hometown crowd was like any other, then the people who helped raise him wanted him to expound the values they held dear. They wanted to know that their investment in him had paid off. They wanted him to make them proud.

Jesus stood up to read, Luke says. He unrolled the scroll of the prophet Isaiah and found the place where the assigned verses were written. Then he read them out loud:

> The Spirit of the Lord is upon me,
> because he has anointed me
> to bring good news to the poor.
> He has sent me to proclaim release to the captives
> and recovery of sight to the blind,
> to let the oppressed go free,
> to proclaim the year of the Lord's favor. (Luke 4:18–19)

This is not a perfect match with Isaiah 61:1, at least not in modern English translations, but the substance is the same: God anoints prophets to speak and act on God's behalf, freeing those who are locked down by poverty, tyranny, lack of vision, or broken hearts. Whatever is holding people down, God means to lift up. Whatever is tearing people apart, God means to mend.

A phrase in the last line of the reading—"the year of the Lord's favor"—would have had special meaning to those in the synagogue that day. It was a direct reference to the jubilee year, described in the book of Leviticus as a divine rebalancing of the economy. Every fiftieth year, the Bible says, slaves shall be freed, prisoners shall be released, debts shall be forgiven, and land sold under pressure shall be returned to its original owner. "You shall proclaim liberty throughout the land to all its inhabitants," reads Leviticus 25:10, a verse with such lasting power to lift the human heart that it was cast into the top of the Liberty Bell in 1752.

When Jesus finished reading the passage, he rolled up the scroll, handed it back to the attendant, and sat down. "The eyes of all in the synagogue were fixed on him," Luke says. Expectations were very high, and Jesus did not disappoint. "Today this scripture has been fulfilled in your hearing," he said.

Starting here, I am going to press "pause" a couple of times, since this is the point at which many Christians stop listening to the story and start running an old tape they have heard a hundred times instead. Before I became a student of the Bible, I was taught that when Jesus said, "Today this scripture has been fulfilled in your hearing," he was telling the people sitting in front of him that he was the Messiah. This infuriated them so much that they hustled him out of the synagogue to go throw him off a cliff. I can still remember the umbrage I took at "the Jews" who were so dead set against Jesus that they could not hear the good news he brought. I say this now to my shame.

Luke's Gospel tells a different story. In the first place, Jesus never said he was the Messiah. He said that God's jubilee was under way. In the second place, the people sitting in front of him *loved* hearing that. "All spoke well of him and were amazed at the gracious words that came from his mouth," Luke says. They turned to one another and said, "Is not this Joseph's son?" They could not believe that the son of someone they knew had turned out so well. It was like being from the pope's hometown.

I know that some Christians interpret the question about Jesus's parentage as an insult. To their ears, it was a way of putting Jesus back in his place as the son of a man instead of the Son of God. This is odd for several reasons, not least of which is that "Son of Man" was Jesus's preferred way of referring to himself. It is also odd to presume ill will in people who just a moment ago spoke well of Jesus and were amazed at the gracious words that came from his mouth. The only sense I can make of it is that such interpreters are looking for something—anything—that might explain what happened next.

What happened next was that Jesus blew his lid. He may have had excellent reasons for doing it, but *he* was the one who turned the congregation against him—first by accusing them of skepticism about him and then by reminding them that God did not belong to them.

"Doubtless you will quote to me this proverb, 'Doctor, cure yourself!'" he said to them, though they quoted no such thing. "And you will say, 'Do here also in your hometown the things that we have heard you did at Capernaum.'" If you believe Jesus was a mind reader—or was really good at reading body language—then his accusations may make perfect sense to you, but no one said anything like that to him out loud. Strictly speaking, it was *Jesus* who turned on the hometown crowd and not the other way around. Right after telling them that God's jubilee was under way, he assumed their distrust of his good news—not their distrust of his divine status, mind you, but their distrust that God was about to act in a decisive way. He was not finished either. "Truly I tell you," he went on, "no prophet is accepted in the prophet's hometown."

This is another good place to pause the old tape, since you might not have noticed that Jesus said "prophet" and not "messiah." As long as he was on a roll, why not accuse the people in front of him of doubting that he was God's anointed one? But Jesus did not say "messiah." He said "prophet," which can change the way you hear what he said after he read the passage from Isaiah: "Today this scripture has been fulfilled in your hearing." That sounds like something a prophet might say: *God's promises are coming true.* But for whatever reason—mind reading, body language, or the prophetic ability to speak the future—Jesus assumed that no one in his hometown believed him. When he looked at the people in front of him, he saw squinty eyes. He saw "prove it" written all over their faces.

I honestly do not know what was going on in Jesus's mind—or in Luke's mind either, as he decided how to tell this story—but what Jesus said next was what drove his listeners to rage. "Here's the truth," he said in so many words. "There were hungry widows right here when it didn't rain for three and a half years and there was famine all through the land, but God didn't send the prophet Elijah to any of them. God sent him to a widow in Sidon. There were also a lot of miserable lepers right here during the time of the prophet Elisha, but he didn't heal any of them. The only person he healed was Naaman the Syrian."

Everyone listening to him would have known these famous stories of God's deliverance. The stories may have been so familiar, in fact, that people had stopped thinking about the widow or the leper as religious strangers. Like the magi, these two had been thoroughly assimilated into the hometown congregation's sacred plot. When Jesus reached back and pulled them into the spotlight again, however, he made a point of their strangeness. Sidon and Syria were foreign countries. Neither the widow nor the leper was an Israelite. They did not speak Israel's language or worship Israel's god when God sent prophets to help them. This might have been all right if God had helped everyone in Israel first, but that was not what God did. In these famous stories of God's deliverance, God chose to help foreigners instead of family. God blessed the strangers and let the family hurt.

"When they heard *this*, all in the synagogue were filled with rage," Luke says (emphasis mine). They were not furious because Jesus had made special claims for himself. They were furious because he had taken a swing at their sense of divine privilege— and he had used their own scriptures to do it.

If the word "synagogue" makes you think this is a story about Jesus and Jews, it is time to press the pause button again. Jesus was in his home congregation. He was among his own people. If he had been a twenty-first century Christian instead, he might have told the members of his home church that God was free to heal a Taliban fighter without lifting a finger to help thousands of wounded American veterans. He might have told them that God could choose to send someone with a bag of groceries to a Hindu widow living in a trailer park without leaving anything on the doorsteps of her hungry Christian neighbors. Until you let that message sink in, you may never understand why the people in Jesus's hometown synagogue wanted to throw him off a cliff or why so many Christians have distorted this extremely upsetting story.

Once, in a minor attempt to preach it straight, I suggested that Christians who wanted to take Jesus's sermon to heart might start by donating some of their outreach funds to a local Muslim community that was trying to buy land for a cemetery or by volunteering at an after-school program at the Laotian Buddhist temple—anything they could think of, really, that might help them mirror God's indiscriminate love. Luckily, I was preaching in a town with no cliffs.

I am not saying that Christians have a hard time caring for those who are not Christian. It happens all the time. A synagogue burns, and local churches take up a collection for the rebuilding fund. A Muslim girl wearing hijab is threatened in public, and Christians step up to protect her. You hear stories like that all the time, for good reason. Putting oneself at risk for the safety of others is a central Christian teaching. So is laying down one's life for one's friends. When Christians act instinctively and self-sacrificially on behalf of those outside the tribe, you can almost hear the angels sing, because someone got the sermon.

But there is a deeper message in the sermon at Nazareth, which is that no one owns God. The great religions may possess genuine revelations of God's nature and purpose. Their most gifted listeners may truly have discerned a divine call to special purpose, both for themselves and for their communities. Traditions that do not speak of God have certainly perceived truths about the human condition and have conceived inspired ways to transcend it. But whatever we mean when we say "God" is not fully captured by any of these traditions. If it could be, it would not be God.

This can be very difficult for some faithful people to accept, especially those who read their sacred texts selectively. Yet one of the reasons these texts are sacred is because of the cautions in them about trying to lay claim to God. When people of faith reach out for God with sticky fingers, their holy books remind them that possessing God's word is not the same thing as possessing God. In a familiar passage from the Hebrew Bible, God warns the people against becoming *too* familiar.

> For my thoughts are not your thoughts,
> nor are your ways my ways, says the LORD.
> For as the heavens are higher than the earth,
> so are my ways higher than your ways
> and my thoughts than your thoughts. (Isa. 55:8–9)

In the Christian New Testament, Jesus himself admits that he does not know everything there is to know about God. When his disciples ask him to tell them about the end times, he gives them a harrowing description that includes everything but *when*. "But about that day or hour no one knows," he says, "neither the angels in heaven, nor the Son, but only the Father."

Passages like these protect God's autonomy, but most of us prefer those that grant us special privilege. For Christians, the most potent one is John 14:6, in which Jesus says, "No one comes to the Father except through me." Here is the bedrock assurance that Christians alone have access to God. But why is this verse more important than one that comes two chapters earlier in John's Gospel? "Whoever believes in me believes not in me but in him who sent me," Jesus says in John 12:44. Maybe my hearing is off, but those two verses sound different to me. So why do so many Christians know the former saying but not the latter one? Could it be that our favorite verses are the ones that make us feel most right?

"I have other sheep that do not belong to this fold." That is something else Jesus says in John's Gospel. He does not elaborate, but I like imagining the God of many sheep, many folds, many favorites, many mansions. This is how far my holy envy has brought me: from fearing that Jesus will be mad at me for smelling other people's roses to trusting that Jesus is the Way that embraces all ways. Because there is only one of me, I can only walk one way at a time, but that does not prevent me from believing that other people might be walking their ways with equal devotion and good will.

No one owns God. God alone knows what is good. For reasons that will never be entirely clear, God has a soft spot for religious strangers, both as agents of divine blessing and recipients of divine grace—to the point that God sometimes chooses one of them over people who believe they should by all rights come first. This is a great mystery, but it does nothing to obscure the great commandment. In every circumstance, regardless of the outcome, the main thing Jesus has asked me to do is to love God and my neighbor as religiously as I love myself. The minute I have that handled, I will ask for my next assignment. For now, my hands are full.

The Shadow-Bearers

O mankind! Truly We created you from a male and a
female, and We made you peoples and tribes that you
may come to know one another. Surely the most noble
of you before God are the most reverent of you. Truly
God is Knowing, Aware.

QUR'AN 49:13

When I ask students to rise from their seats during the first
week of Religion 101 and write what they already know
about the religions we will study on the board, I can predict
what they will write under Islam. "Terrorism" will lead the list;
"Muhammad," "9/11," "Allah," "ISIS," "veiled women," "Saudi
Arabia," and "the Qur'an" will show up somewhere underneath.
This helps explain why some Muslim students decide not to add
anything more nuanced to the list. They can see which way the
wind is blowing. I remember one in particular, a winsome young
man with roots in Mali. He asked me not to ask him about being
Muslim in class, since he was not ready for his classmates to see
him "that way."

It was not always so. When I first began teaching the class,
Islam was only a little more foreign than the other religions on

the course plan. The first, failed attack on the World Trade Center in 1993 had receded in memory, leaving most students with the impression that Islam was a religion in the Middle East whose combative followers had brown skin, lived in the desert, and wore flowing white gowns. Few could have guessed that Indonesia has the largest Muslim population in the world or that the majority of Muslims are not Arab. Fewer still would have suspected that Muslims revere Jesus or that the Qur'an upholds his virgin birth and says more about his mother than the New Testament does.

The hardest thing to remember is that most of these students were still in diapers when the second, successful attack on the World Trade Center took place in 2001. The United States has been at war in one Muslim country or another ever since. Hardly a day goes by without headlines involving troops, coups, bombings, or body counts. Hollywood, Washington, and Wall Street have all capitalized on the fear generated by terrorist attacks at home and abroad. Trying to teach Islam under this sky full of thunderheads is like trying to teach Christianity at the height of the Thirty Years' War, in which more than eight million Christians died.

I have six class sessions in which to give students something better for their imaginations to work with. I started out with four—the same number as all of the other religions we study—but the unit on Islam was so full of difficulties that I stretched it out, so we could at least name some of the problems. On the first day of the unit I write them on the board:

- Recognizing the entanglement of politics, economics, history, and religion
- Noticing how religions change from culture to culture
- Vetting the viewpoints of your news sources

✸ Resisting the tendency to judge the many by the
  actions of the few
✸ Understanding the dynamics of your own fear

The last one is such a sleeper that I sometimes wonder if Psychology 101 should be a prerequisite for Religion 101, but the truth is that all of these difficulties are embedded in the study of every religion. The only reason to tag them during the study of Islam is because they are lying right on top, easy to identify in controversies ranging from the veiling of women in the United States to the armed conflict between Syria and Iraq. But what are two extra class sessions compared to the weight of world news, hate speech on the web, the typecasting of TV villains with Middle Eastern accents, and the easy pass given to those who speak ill of Islam? Where are students supposed to get better information about ordinary Muslims who suffer from the actions of the few both at home and abroad?

When I read a study that says 38 percent of Americans know someone who is Muslim,[1] I test the statistic with a hand-raise in class. The figure is way too high for Piedmont students. So few of them know a single Muslim that there is no compelling reason for them to doubt the images they have gotten from a screen. If they learn something interesting in class and share it with a friend or family member, they risk being shut down by those who know nothing of Islam except what they hear on the news. "What, so you think it's interesting that people who kidnap young girls and make them sex slaves also pray five times a day? You need to drop that class before you get recruited by ISIS." A student actually repeated that comment by her father to me.

I call it "the worst-case conversation stopper," a technique that works on almost any subject. You try to have a conversation with another mother about letting your fifth-grade daughters walk six blocks to school together, and she cites the unsolved murder of a girl in another state who was last seen walking to school. You try to have a conversation with your gym buddy about guns in church, and he asks you if you really want the next shooter to be the only guy in the room with a gun.

It is hard to argue with worst-case scenarios, especially those that have really happened. At the same time, allowing them to freeze-frame the discussion can put you in a code-orange state of readiness for a life that is—for most of the readers of this book anyway—largely shades of green. The last time I rode under the sign that keeps track of highway fatalities in Georgia, I realized that I was in far greater danger of dying in a traffic accident than I was of dying in a terrorist attack. That is an indelicate comparison, I know, but it points to the difference between mortal fear and terror. Most people's fear of a drunk driver or a texting teenager does not spill over onto everyone they meet, but their fear of a terrorist does. Every Muslim becomes a suspect, or at least the ones who meet the stereotype of what a Muslim looks like. Even those who do not—the optometrist at Walmart, for instance, or the saleswoman at Nordstrom who tries to talk you into a shorter hemline—become used to hearing people say libelous things about them every single day, because of worst-case scenarios that terrify them as badly as anyone else.

What must it be like to live like that? How does such constant scorn affect your faith? How do you teach your children to ignore what other people say about you and the things you hold most sacred? Since I am a Southerner with vivid memories of the American civil rights movement, it is easy to come up with a parallel set of questions. How do you deal with the deadly hostility of people who think they know everything about you simply by looking at you? How do you change a mind that knows nothing about its own shadows?

Because white men can't
police their imagination
black men are dying.

These are three lines from *Citizen: An American Lyric* by the poet Claudia Rankine. When a British journalist asked her what was in her mind when she wrote it, Rankine said, "When white men are shooting black people, some of it is malice and some an out-of-control image of blackness in their minds.[2] In the same way, I believe, there is an out-of-control image of Islam in many minds that has little to do with ordinary Muslims, who serve as the shadow-bearers for people with no wish or will to explore their own shadows.

Though most of my students are too young to remember 9/11, I remember it well. It was a Tuesday. I was in my office collating handouts on the Five Pillars of Islam. A field trip to a historic masjid in Atlanta was coming up on Friday, and students always had a lot of questions about what to expect. When the telephone rang I debated letting it go to voicemail, since class began in a few minutes, but the phone rang so seldom I picked it up. It was my husband Ed, telling me that a plane had just crashed into one of the World Trade Center Towers in Manhattan.

"Are you near a television?" he said. "You really should take a look."

"I will," I said. "Right after class."

By Thursday I had checked with the dean to make sure the Friday field trip could go ahead. I had called the masjid to make sure there would be extra security guards on duty. The dean said we were good to go. Remembering all of that now tells me how much the culture of terror has grown over the years. Under the same circumstances, would I press for such a field trip now? No, I would not. I would cancel the trip, and everyone would understand why. Yet three days after the largest terrorist attack in US history, I and everyone I spoke to felt reasonably sure that it was safe to take college students to a large masjid in a major city. All that remained was to find out if anyone still wanted to go.

First the students and I processed the events of the past week as best we could. Then I passed around the sign-up sheet for the field trip, which had sixteen names on it. When it came back to me, half of them were crossed off. In the end, eight of us went to the Atlanta Masjid of Al-Islam for Friday prayers. When we arrived, close to six hundred people were jammed into a room that held radio and newspaper reporters as well as worshippers. The women students and I sat in the back, while the two men students sat nearer the front. As more and more people spilled into the room, ushers motioned us forward to make room for others.

There is something about sitting on the floor with your shoes off that can calm you right down. I did not know how the students in the men's section were feeling, but back in the women's section things were pretty cozy. We were sitting shoulder to shoulder with our stocking feet sticking out in front of us. There were a couple of babies crawling around, and no one was scolding them. A couple of the students leaned against each other. Two others fooled around with each other's scarves. It was like waiting for a concert to begin, with so many new things to look at that the mind stayed present in a room where anything could happen next.

At 2:00 p.m. sharp the muezzin stood to give the call to prayer. His voice settled the crowd. One of the babies stopped crawling and sat down, looking up at his mother to see if she was making the sound. The students stopped fidgeting too. I had been to the masjid before, but they had not. I hoped they were managing their anxiety. Mine was focused on what the imam would say and how the crowd would react. His name was Plemon El-Amin. He had been at the masjid a long time. He was known in Atlanta as a bridge-builder and peacemaker, which helped explain the media presence. His job, like the job of every imam standing up to speak that Friday, was to address the pressing issues of the day and advise believers on how their faith should inform their lives. I wondered how much sleep he had gotten since Tuesday.

El-Amin began in the customary way, praising God and calling the congregation to attention in Arabic. Then he spoke in English, citing a teaching from the prophet Muhammad that "the ink of the scholar is more holy than the blood of the martyr." In the hour that followed he spoke directly to my condition, though I have only my memory to rely on now. The actions of the hijackers exposed the falseness of their claim to being Muslims, he said. The only sympathy possible for them was the sympathy one might have for people who have lost their minds. Returning to his text, he explained that the long lineage of Muslim scholars who have worked collaboratively for centuries to interpret the Qur'an in the most humane ways are more to be trusted than those who spill blood based on their own readings and ambitions.

The longer he talked, the deeper I breathed. I could not see the students' faces both because of the scarves and because their eyes were fixed on him. They leaned forward, not back, hooking their arms around their knees. The imam did not say anything to stoke our fear or provoke our anger. He called us back to compassion, to peace, to trust in God. He told us how important it was to partner with those of other faiths to resist violence in our communities in the days to come. I say "us" and "our" because he made me feel like part of his congregation. Everything he said went straight to my ransacked heart. He was my Melchizedek.

The Friday service ended as it always does, with congregational prayer. As soon as people started standing up, I led the women students off to the side of the room, hoping the men students remembered to do the same thing. Then we watched the Muslims draw near each other, lining up in straight rows with their toes touching the toes of the people on either side of them. A bunch of grandmothers sat with babies on their laps in a row of chairs along the back wall. A woman in a wheelchair to my right reached down to set her brakes.

When the imam gave the word, the Muslims bowed with their hands crossed over their bodies, then dropped to their knees and pressed their heads to the ground. A woman with a toddler sheltered her child beneath her body. The woman in the wheelchair tipped as far forward as she could without falling out. When everyone repeated the movement a moment later, it was like watching a huge, perfect wave curl and fall with a rush toward the shore.

Then it was over. Someone stepped up to the microphone and started making announcements. Reporters surrounded the imam, while women in bright headscarves did the same thing to the students and me. Some patted our backs or shoulders and asked us our names. Others embraced us or kissed us on both cheeks. "You came to see for yourself," one woman said after she had stepped back from hugging me. "With so many wrong ideas about us, so many false reports—you came to see for yourself."

In years to come I would return to that masjid again and again, not only to let students experience that kind of welcome, but also to learn what I could from the imam about how to speak from my own faith to people of other faiths in such a powerful way. I envied that. But President Bush had said something on 9/11 that turned out to be prophetic, and not in a good way. In his address to the nation on the night of the attacks, he said, "The pictures of airplanes flying into buildings, fires burning, and huge structures collapsing have filled us with disbelief, terrible sadness, and a quiet, unyielding anger." All these years later, the unyielding anger is still there. If anything, it has gotten worse.

On the day we discuss in class why Judaism, Christianity, and Islam are all called Abrahamic religions, one student is eager to share what she knows about Abraham's household. Terrorism is God's lasting judgment on Abraham for sleeping with his wife's maid, she says. If he had not slept with Hagar, there would be no such thing as Islam and the world would be a safer place.

"Who told you that?" I ask.

"My preacher," she says.

Another student tells me that her pastor has launched a sermon series called "The Star, the Crescent, and the Cross." Troubled by what he has seen and heard about Islamic terrorism, the pastor has decided to read the Qur'an all the way through, so he can tell his congregation what it really says. He does not read Arabic. He does not understand that Muslims do not the read the Qur'an the same way he reads the Bible. He is unaware of *tafsir*, the Arabic word for "exegesis," which points to the long tradition of scholarly interpretation of the Qur'an. He does not ask a Muslim friend to help him understand what he is reading. He simply downloads an English translation of the Qur'an and begins to read—first from the beginning and then, when he finds the first chapter too tedious, from the shorter chapters at the end.

In his first sermon he says that he is only three-quarters of the way through, but he has read enough to assure his congregation that, wherever they pick it up, the Qur'an is "one long droning of what Allah expects, and if you don't turn to him, he's going to give you incredibly painful divine retribution." The pastor says a great deal more than that—all of it available on podcast—but his bottom line is that "these people have made themselves your enemy—the enemy of the cross." This does not give his listeners license to make enemies of Muslims, he says, to his credit, but it does mean that they should expect attacks on non-Muslims to continue, since "the Qur'an incites people to violence."

When I hear things like that, I feel like I am bailing water out of a rowboat made from newspaper and spit. How can I possibly persuade students at a time like this that Islam is as rich and corruptible as any other religion? How can I teach them to deconstruct what they hear? It does not help that the Muslim world is in conflict on three continents. That this has as much to do with geopolitics as religion is of little interest to people in their early twenties. Most have no idea that the US backed fundamentalist Afghan *mujahedin* during the war with the Soviets in the 1980s, or supported Saddam Hussein's forces during the Iran-Iraq war of those same years. These are shadow stories that even I have a hard time hearing. There is also the age-old problem of sibling rivalry. The Abrahamic religions belong to a complicated blended family in which our similarities provoke as much friction as our differences.

In his significant book *Not in God's Name*, Jonathan Sacks reverses a popular trope. It is not our religion that makes us violent, he says. Instead, it is our penchant for violence that gives rise to our religious impulse. People are born with two sets of primal instincts, he notes: altruism toward those in our own group and aggression toward others.[3] In daily life, this dynamic shows up in everything from football rivalry and political affiliation to racial division and armed combat.

Since most of us need to feel good about ourselves while we are acting aggressively toward others, we develop psychological mechanisms such as splitting, projection, and scapegoating, which allow us to assign goodness to our group and badness to the other group. This not only relieves us of having to deal with the goodness and badness inside our own group; it also frees us to believe that our violence against the other group is essentially altruistic. We bond best with our group when we confront an external enemy.

Sacks exposes another illusion when he points out that historical substitutes for religion have done greater harm than religion. These include the nationalism that sparked two world wars, the ideological system that gave Mao and Stalin license to murder millions of their own people, and the racism that fueled the Holocaust. "After that," Sacks writes, "no one who argues that abolishing religion will lead to peace can be taken seriously."[4] It is neither our secularism nor our religion that fuels our violence, he concludes, but our fundamental "groupishness."

By the time the students have finished six class sessions on Islam, they know how much Jews, Christians, and Muslims have in common: not just Abraham, but also Moses, the commandments, the prophets, the holy city of Jerusalem, charity, fasting, pilgrimage, prayer, sacred texts, sacred washing, justice, free will, care for neighbors, angels, the coming messiah, the day of judgment, the resurrection of the dead, and—sooner or later—participation in the eternal life of the one God. Everything on that long list belongs at the center of what the three religions share.

The biggest surprise for everyone is that Christians and Muslims both revere Jesus. Muslims call him Isa, believing him to be both prophet and messiah. Christians believe he shares divine status with God, which neither Jews nor Muslims can affirm, but Muslims honor him as an exemplar of what it means to truly surrender to God. Contrary to popular opinion, Muslims and Christians can both wear "I ❤ Jesus" T-shirts and mean it.

Letting this sink in for the first time, I am struck by the realization that Christians do not own Jesus any more than we own God. He has other sheep who do not belong to our fold, and when he is walking with them, they see him very differently. Hindus may see him in the saffron robes of a holy man or as an avatar who manifests the divine. Buddhists see him sitting in the lotus position as a bodhisattva, a compassionate being who works for the benefit of all beings. Jews have every reason to see him as the shepherd of a murderous flock, though there are a few who can see him as a liberal Pharisee of his day or a passionate rabbi who died for his vision of Judaism.

The most interesting Jewish view of him that I come across is the idea of Jesus as a failed messiah—not false, but failed—who said and did all the right things but who could not achieve the final goal of bringing God's kingdom to earth. The Jerusalem temple was destroyed a generation after his death. The lion did not lie down with the lamb. Yet this messiah son of Joseph, as one Jewish writer calls him, suffered and died to prepare the way for the final redemption to take place.[5]

Jesus may not have been a Christian, but Christians do not like anyone else claiming to know him as well as we do. When the Muslim scholar Reza Aslan wrote *Zealot: The Life and Times of Jesus of Nazareth* in 2013, Christian backlash was swift and heated. Since I have not read the book, I cannot comment, except to say that it is interesting how many of the Christians who objected to Aslan's speaking of Jesus believe they are competent to speak of Muhammad. What happened to the Golden Rule?

In recent years I have begun taking students on a weekday tour of a large downtown masjid instead of to Friday prayers. There are two reasons for this. The first is that I find it increasingly awkward to bring spectators to other people's worship. The second is that I read about a teacher who got in big trouble when he took his class on a field trip to a mosque and someone made a video of several of his students taking part in the prayers. The video became part of a larger attack on the mosque, which boomeranged back on the school.[6] It was a public middle school, not a private college, but why tempt fate? By taking students for a Wednesday tour instead of Friday prayers, I can handle both of my concerns.

On the day I am remembering, the students and I arrive a little early in spite of the fact that the women have spent a lot of time looking in the rearview mirrors of the school van to make sure their borrowed scarves cover their hair. Some like wearing the scarves so much that they do not want to give them back at the end. Others never stop fuming about how the scarves make them feel silenced, sidelined, and oppressed. In this way, they are not so different from young women who happen to be Muslim. Some fight to wear the hijab; others fight not to wear it. Since my job is to be a perfect stranger, I knot the ends of my scarf behind my neck and lead the way to the front door of the masjid.

It is a magnificent building in midtown Atlanta with two schools on its campus, which helps explain why we run into a crowd of young boys in ankle-length white robes coming out of the masjid as we are going in. A few of them turn smiling faces toward us while the rest flow between us engrossed in their own conversations. Once inside, we take off our shoes and place them in cubbyholes, feeling the coolness of the marble floor under our feet. Then we wait for our host to appear.

I have met a variety of guides over the years—all men—who have graciously agreed to meet my group at the masjid. One was so white that he looked like my Uncle Howard. Another was a Pan-Africanist who converted to Islam during the Vietnam War. One was a Pakistani physician, and another was a retired real-estate agent from I don't remember where. Since they were all citizens of the United States, I have to wonder why I remain so curious about their origins. Edward Said, a groundbreaking scholar and cultural critic of the last century, called it "Orientalism"—the way Westerners like myself persist in thinking of Near Eastern cultures as exotically "other."

Today's host greets us a few moments later, introducing himself by name and asking us ours. He is a doctor who has taken time out of his practice to fulfill one of the missions of the masjid: "Presenting Islam to the followers of other faiths and promoting goodwill between Muslims and non-Muslims," as the website says.[7] I have met him before. Years earlier, when the pastor of a fifty-member church in Florida made national news by threatening to burn a Qur'an (which he later did), a student asked the doctor how he felt about that.

"Well," he said, "of course I was dismayed at first, since I knew how much trouble it would cause." Then, improbably, he smiled. "But then I thought I might write Pastor Jones and ask if he planned to burn old Qur'ans or new ones—because we have some very old ones here, and if he would be willing to send us some new ones then perhaps we could work out a mutually beneficial exchange." He was not serious, of course, but his ability to turn a hostile threat into a joke impressed the students as much as anything else he said.

Now he leads us through a pair of very tall doors into the main prayer hall of the masjid. This surprises me since the women's prayer room is upstairs behind glass panels, and there are men praying in this hall, but he points to some folding chairs leaning against the wall and invites us to set them up in a circle. We do, with as little clanking as possible. Then we all sit down, the women tugging at their scarves and the men tilting their heads to look at the elaborate patterns inside the great dome of the roof.

The doctor speaks for about thirty minutes about the central teachings of Islam. Then he takes questions from the students, most of which he has answered a hundred times before.

"Why do the women have to sit up there?"

"Why did we have to take our shoes off?"

"Why don't Muslims believe in Jesus?"

"Is it true you can have four wives?"

When a student asks our host what it is like to be Muslim in the United States today, he pauses. "It is more difficult now," he says, knowing that we have no way of measuring the distance between his "then" and his "now." "Let us say that when I travel overseas, I always leave several hours early for the airport, so that when I am detained I will not miss my flight." He does not say "if" he is detained. He says "when."

After a few more questions, a student asks whether it is possible to purchase a Qur'an. The doctor gets up, goes over to a bookcase against the wall, picks up a cardboard box, and sets it down on an empty chair in the circle.

"Please, help yourselves," he says. "Since there is no compulsion in religion for Muslims, I will not hand you a copy, but you are free to pick one up if you like." Almost all of the students take him up on the offer, weighing the books in their hands like contraband as they make their way back to the college van. Remembering the uproar at the University of North Carolina a few years back when incoming students were assigned to read a book on the Qur'an, I am glad that I work at Piedmont.[8]

On the last day of the unit on Islam, I turn on the overhead projector and let students watch Nina Davuluri perform the Bollywood dance routine that helped her become Miss America 2014. Born in Syracuse, New York, to Hindu parents from southeast India, Davuluri was the first American of Indian descent to win the Miss America competition. Within moments of the announcement, Twitter erupted.

"I am literally soo mad right now a ARAB won Miss America," reads one.

"So miss america is a terrorist," reads another.

"Miss America? You mean Miss 7–11," reads a third, a reference to how many 7-Eleven stores are owned or staffed by Indian Americans.

By now the anti-Muslim comments have given way to anti-brown sentiments, as in a final tweet that says, "Asian or indian are you kiddin this is america omg."[9]

I do not have to say much after that. Students shift uncomfortably in their seats, recognizing things that have shown up on their own Twitter feeds. They may not remember everything they have learned about mainstream Islam, but they know how race, religion, and social class get all mixed up in people's minds. Now that they have seen how ugly it can get, they do not want to be the kind of people who take part in it any more. Though the self-protective benefits of "groupishness" may never go away, they have gained a glimpse of the world through other eyes that they will have a hard time forgetting.

It will still take enormous energy for them to keep this glimpse from sinking under the weight of the twenty-four-hour news cycle. If they stay tuned for even an hour of it, the media will download image upon image to their heads: Muslim faces misshapen with rage, running from something in the back-ground from which smoke is spiraling up, or carrying a home-made coffin surrounded by veiled women who are beating their breasts with fists. In the face of such a tragic picture gallery it is hard to mount an argument that this is a curated fraction of the truth. Where can I get photos to back up my claim that most people of every faith wish to live in peace? What are my sources for believing that I have nothing to fear from the vast majority of people who do not share my faith? My only hope—the small hope embedded in this book—is that the students in Religion 101 will be able to maintain possession of their own imagina-tions, declining to surrender them to people who know nothing about their life, their school, their faith, or their friends of many faiths.

The faces on the news are real and important. I want never to forget how much other people in other parts of the world are suffering from groupishness in all its deadly forms. At the same time, I want never to let those faces obscure the faces of the people in my near world who have kissed me on both cheeks, preached peace to me from an Arabic text, been students in my classes, welcomed me into their sacred spaces, invited me to break their fast with them, smiled up at me in their long white robes, showed me how to tie a head scarf so it would stay put, and reminded me that the neighbors God has given me to love do not all call God by the same name.

It is possible that my attitude is naive. I have been told that. I have also been told that I am going to hell for it. Since it is Jesus's turn in the classroom next, I will wait and see what he says this time. The only religion left on the course plan is my own, which will give me one more chance to figure out just how Christian I really am.

Failing Christianity

This is my song, O God of all the nations,
a song of peace for lands afar and mine;
this is my home, the country where my heart is;
here are my hopes, my dreams, my holy shrine:
but other hearts in other lands are beating
with hopes and dreams as true and high as mine.

CHRISTIAN HYMN BY LLOYD STONE

Time has just run out for the ten-point quiz on Christianity. Students who finished quizzes on other religions in record time are still sitting in their seats, staring at the multiple-choice questions on Christian origins, sacred texts, and central beliefs and practices. Since the same thing happened to me in college, I know what they are doing. They are making bargains with the God of Tests. They are promising that they will study harder next time in return for any kind of rescue right now. They are convincing themselves that if they do not blink, the correct answer will begin to glow on the paper in front of them, making it impossible to ignore.

"Time's up," I say. When no one moves, I try again.

"Really," I say, pointing to the clock on the wall. "It's time to go. Make sure your name is on your quiz, and I'll see you Thursday."

"I think I just did the worst on my own religion," one student says as she drops her paper on the pile. A young man behind her asks me if Constantine was the main figure in the Protestant Reformation and slaps his forehead when I break the bad news. The only student who makes an A+ on the Christianity quiz is Shlomo, the orthodox Jew, perhaps because he is the only one who knew he had to study for it.

The first time this happened, I did not see it coming. I knew that the unit on Christianity would be *different* for students, since it was the religion they knew the most about. I just did not think it would be so *difficult* for them to approach a familiar faith the same way they had approached the others: from the outside, not the inside.

"I couldn't hold on to what I was learning in class," one student says when she gets her quiz back. "I found it incredibly interesting, but I couldn't make it stay in my head. It was so different from what I had already learned that my brain just kept switching back." As she speaks, I imagine her in front of her mental file cabinet with her class notes in her hand. The labels on the drawers say, "Sunday School," "Bible Study," "Youth Group," and "Personal Relationship with Christ." Those drawers hold important, life-giving things, but where is she supposed to put her new insight about the role of the early churches in the formation of the New Testament? Where does she put her new awareness of the Eastern Orthodox Church? The problem is not that her drawers are full. The problem is that none of the labels on them match what is in her hand.

Over the years I have met students who could recite the sixty-six names of the books of the Bible in order, but had no idea how or when those books were assembled into a sacred library. Some grew up with parents and grandparents who were Baptist ministers, but they never knew that made them Protestants until they learned it in class. Fewer and fewer have heard of the Nicene Creed. Most are surprised to learn that early Christians believed baptism was supposed to be a one-time thing or that sprinkling was an acceptable method.

When they discover that the Gospels of Matthew and Luke tell significantly different stories of Jesus's birth, this astonishes them only slightly less than discovering that the Gospels of Mark and John tell no such stories at all. When they find out that Paul was not one of the original twelve disciples, they cannot remember why they thought he was. No one ever told them about Constantine, Augustine, Charlemagne, Pope Leo IX, or Martin Luther, and some are not persuaded that they need to know about them now. What happened in the centuries between Jesus's resurrection and their own profession of faith is of little relevance in the churches where most of them grew up. They were raised to take their places in line directly behind the disciples, picking up the proclamation of the gospel where those simple fishermen left off.

So it is no wonder they do not know where to file what they learn in class, especially since many find the new information unsettling. If the contents of the New Testament were not set in stone until the fourth century, what did early Christians read? Why do some Bibles have a section between the Old and New Testaments called the Apocrypha, and others do not? If the most ancient copies of Mark's Gospel end halfway through the last chapter—before anyone has seen the risen Christ—then who wrote the longer ending in their Bibles? That is the part with snake handling in it, which increases their investment in the answer.

There is little time to linger over discussions like these, since we only have four class sessions for Christianity. It is one of the things that gives me a pain in the side: in a survey course like this one, the easy questions are the ones that get answered. The hard ones—the important ones—are too often deferred. I find them written on the index cards I leave strewn around the room for questions the students have not had time to ask in class (or do not want to ask out loud).

> "Is the God of the New Testament a different God from the God of the Old Testament? If so, why do Christians say they believe in one God?"

> "Who decided what books would be in the New Testament? Was that a decision made by God or men?"

> "My boyfriend is Mormon, and he says he is Christian. Some of my Christian friends say he's not. Who is right?"

Since my first college religion class took place in the last millennium, my questions were different, but I still remember the almost physical rush of being denied easy answers. My religion professor was not interested in teaching me what to think. He wanted to teach me *how* to think, which was so different from what I expected that I kept signing up for religion courses until I had enough to declare a major.

Part of my good fortune was the emptiness of my religious file cabinet. When I arrived at college I had attended various churches with friends. I had been baptized by immersion when I was sixteen, but that had more to do with my boyfriend than with God. I did not grow up with Christian teachings. I cannot

remember ever saying a prayer with my family around the dinner table. There were no Bibles in my house except the pocket
New Testament with the white leatherette cover that my grandmother gave me when I was ten.

By the time I got to college, I had devotion but very few beliefs. I had not stayed long enough in any of the churches I visited
to receive full indoctrination. Even the preacher who baptized
me did not ask for a meeting ahead of time to make sure I understood what I was doing. He just put on his hip waders and
met me in the baptismal pool, where I was so tall that he almost
toppled over when he bent me backward into the water. That
was the last I saw of him, at least at eye level. I gathered from
his sermons that Jesus had forgiven us for our sins, though he
continued to berate us for them. When my boyfriend joined the
army, I moved on.

In a reversal of the usual pattern, my real conversion to
Christianity started in the classroom—in my college textbooks,
in the things my professors asked me to think about, in the papers I wrote for them. That was how I learned my way around
the Trinity, the social gospel, the Christian mystics, and the Hebrew prophets. Though it may be unkind to say so, I had never
thought of Christians as particularly bright people. In college I
learned how *smart* they could be, which made me want to be one
of them more than anything else.

I started attending university worship. I became a religion major. I applied to seminary and was accepted, though
I did not belong to a church and had heard no call from God.
It was not until I decided to become an Episcopalian at the
age of twenty-five that I became fully and willingly indoctri-
nated into Christian belief. I accepted the doctrines of original
sin, the incarnation of God in Christ, his divine partnership

with the Father and the Holy Spirit, his redemptive death on
the cross, his resurrection from the dead, his second coming,
and the unity of his church. When ordination followed several years later, I accepted the responsibility of communicating
those same truths to the congregations I served with as much
confidence and intelligence as I could.

Then I left parish ministry for teaching religion at the college
level. As unexpected as this turn of events was, it proved the
truth of a frequently quoted line from T. S. Eliot's poetry. I arrived where I had started and knew the place for the first time.
I was back in a college classroom much like the one where I had
learned to love Christianity. Now it was my turn to deny students easy answers. It was my chance to see if I could ignite their
minds and quicken their spirits at the same time. When it came
to the unit on Christianity, my dilemma was much the same as
theirs. I too had to look at my religion from the outside as well
as the inside and be prepared to lose my balance during the spin.

My belief in the unity of the church was the first thing to
go. Like most Christians I had long spoken of "the Church"—
capital C—as if it were one instead of many. I warmed to the
biblical image of the Church as Christ's body—one being with
many members, dependent on one another for fullness of life.
When I was a pastor, my favorite service in *The Book of Common
Prayer* was Holy Baptism, which begins like this:

Celebrant	There is one Body and one Spirit;
People	There is one hope in God's call to us;
Celebrant	One Lord, one Faith, one Baptism;
People	One God and Father of all.

Perhaps I was better at thinking metaphorically then. Or perhaps I had the Episcopal faith in mind when I said, "one Faith."
Even I had been baptized more than once. But I was not vetting
the words as I went. I just loved the sound of them, the way they
made me feel. As Christians have long proclaimed, I coasted on
the assurance that our unity was real in heaven even when it was
nowhere to be found on earth.

Once I began teaching Christianity in a college classroom
instead of a Sunday school room, the tension between heaven
and earth became more fraught. The Great Schism between the
Eastern and Western churches in the eleventh century struck me
as a very big deal, especially since it goes on dividing Christians
to this day. So does the bloody divorce between Catholic and
Protestant Christians in the sixteenth century. In class I soft-
ened these ruptures by teaching the students what I had been
taught: these historical divisions explain how the three branches
of the Christian Church came to be. The one Church includes
Catholic, Orthodox, and Protestant Christians, who are united
by one Lord, one faith, one baptism.

Imagine my surprise, then, when I discovered that the Roman Catholic and Eastern Orthodox Churches both reject the
"branch theory" of the Church, which they view as an inven-
tion by the Church of England. This helped me understand why
I believed it, since the Episcopal Church descended from the
Church of England. But I could not have been more surprised to
learn that I was not part of the one true Church, which both the
Roman Catholic and Eastern Orthodox churches claim to repre-
sent. I do not bring this up now in order to foment more dissent.
It just seems helpful to admit that Christianity is as complicated
and conflicted as any other religion, with groups of followers
who can believe in the unity of their faith even as they refuse

Communion to one another. Poor Jesus. How does the body survive when there is no circulation in the feet?

The historical record became personal for me when I attended my ninety-one-year-old uncle's funeral in Texas, knowing full well there would be limits on my participation since I am not Catholic. This happened after I had been teaching for fifteen years, which means I was fully aware of the reasons why Christians of good faith might not take Communion together or recognize the validity of each other's ordinations. I did not wear a clergy collar to the funeral. I declined the invitation to say a few words at the end. I had been an Episcopal priest for thirty years by then. The Catholic priest who led the service had been ordained a little more than three.

I met his eyes when he reminded the congregation that only Catholics took Communion in the Catholic Church, which was easy to do since he was looking straight at me. He asked those of us who were not Catholic to please respect their tradition, and I did. I really did. I even believed I was theologically prepared for what was coming next, but as I watched people who had known my uncle for less than a year going up to the altar rail for bread and wine while I sat in my pew with my hands folded in my lap, I felt the full sting of my exclusion. By the time I followed the coffin out of the church, I no longer believed in the unity of the church. Christians are as divided from one another as we are from people of different faiths.

By the next day I could own this as a liberating insight, especially since I did not write it off to human sinfulness. Well, some of it I did. But I did not view my uncle's church as sinful, any more than I viewed my own church as sinful for insisting that only baptized Christians may take part in Communion. Every church I can think of has some way of distinguishing "us" from "them," even if it is only asking the ushers to keep an eye on people who come in wearing leather motorcycle jackets with metal studs. Unless I want to separate myself from everyone who does not see things the way I do—which my faith urges me *not* to do—then I have to admit that there are mutually exclusive views of what it means to be Christian and that God alone is smart enough to decide which is best. This frees me to be with Christians who are not like me as well as those who are.

Students always want to know what Jews believe about this or Buddhists believe about that. When we get to the unit on Christianity, I turn the question around on them:

What do Christians believe happens in the Lord's Supper?

At what age do Christians believe people should be baptized?

Do Christians believe in evolution?

Do Christians support stem-cell research?

What is the Christian position on carrying arms in church?

What do Christians believe about the bishop of Rome, the gifts of the Holy Spirit, the celibacy of clergy, or the leadership of women?

The only sensible answer to any of these questions begins with another question: "Which Christians?" There are a lot of waves in the Christian ocean. When you have met one Christian, you have met exactly one.

I stopped capitalizing "the church" after my uncle's funeral—not from cynicism or revenge, but from the wish to be accurate. There are very many Christian churches, with very many different teachings about what it means to be Christian. Accepting those differences seems the least that a teacher of world religions can do. The key noun is plural, not singular. I do not capitalize "the religion" either.

The second major thing that shifted for me in the classroom was my view of Christian evangelism. I had never warmed to the evangelists in my life, but I accepted the sincerity of their efforts. They believed it was their duty, based on a verse at the very end of Matthew's Gospel: "Go therefore and make disciples of all nations, baptizing them in the name of the Father and of the Son and of the Holy Spirit." Biblical scholars raise reasonable questions about the authenticity of that verse as well as its translation into English, but since I knew that would be of limited interest to those with eyes on the prize of my soul, I learned to deflect their spiritual advances the same way I dealt with telephone solicitors. I told them I knew they had a job to do, that I already had enough of what they were selling, and to please take me off their call lists.

It was not until I began meeting people of other faiths in their most sacred spaces that I learned how bruised some of them were by Christian evangelism. Worshippers at the Hindu Temple returned to the parking lot after one of their major festivals to find Christians by their cars with pamphlets demeaning their holiday. Muslims were used to Christians saying malicious things about the Qur'an. Native Americans were tired of being asked what God they prayed to. The shared consensus is that Christian evangelists are not very good listeners. They assume they are speaking to people with no knowledge of God themselves. They are disrespectful of other people's faith.

Once, on a trip to Central America, I stood at the airport waiting to collect my luggage with a local guide named Gustavo. While we stood watching the carousel go around and around, I heard him groan as if someone had just pulled the wheel of a big suitcase over his foot.

"What's the matter?" I asked, following his line of sight to the crowd of teenagers who had just come through the arrivals door. They were wearing matching T-shirts that had the name of their church on the front and "Bringing the World to Christ" on the back.

"Nothing," he said.

"No, really," I said. "What's the matter?"

"I just wish they would go home," he said. "If they really want to help, they should come two by two, like the Bible says, with nothing but the shoes on their feet. When they come into a village, they should go ask the elders if there is anything for them to do. If the elders cannot think of anything, they should leave. Otherwise we are just characters in their play."

Pearl Buck, the Nobel Prize–winning daughter of Protestant missionaries, said almost the same thing in a book she wrote near the end of her life. Thinking back on people like her parents, she said that even as a child she knew intuitively they were not in China because they loved the Chinese.

No, they were there, these missionaries, to fulfill some spiritual need of their own. It was a noble need, its purposes unselfish, partaking doubtless of that divine need through which God so loved the world that He sent His only begotten Son for its salvation. But somewhere I had learned from Thoreau, who doubtless learned it from Confucius, that if a man comes to do his own good for you, then must you flee that man and save yourself.[1]

Thinking of Pearl growing up in China made me remember a large map of the world I had seen on the wall at a Presbyterian seminary. The age of the frame suggested a date in the last century. So did the names of some of the countries, but it was the coloration of the map that caught my attention. There were bright spots of color in Europe and North Africa. The east coast of North America was a pretty shade of blue and large parts of South America were painted red, but most of the rest of the world was one big expanse of mud brown.

At first I thought it was an unfinished map, begun by someone who had then lost interest—or worse yet, who had dropped dead before he finished adding all the colors. Then I stepped closer and saw "Heathen" written across all the brown parts. Trying to make sense of that, I searched for the legend of the map and found it lower down in the middle under the map title, "The Protestant Missionary Map of the World, 1846." According to the legend, the six colors on the map indicated the dominant religion of each region: blue for Protestant, red for Roman Catholic, pink for Greek, and yellow for Muslim. That last was a surprise, since Judaism did not rate a color at all. Some tiny green spots marked areas of "Decayed Christian Churches." Everything else was brown. "Heathen" was sufficient to describe the ancient wisdom of the Hindu Vedas, the Four Noble Truths of Buddhism, the Torah and Talmud of the Jews, the Tao of the Chinese, and the teachings of Confucius.

I know it is not fair to judge that map by today's standards.

There was no radio in 1846, no telephone, no television, no World Wide Web. There was not even a state of Israel. Today we have all those things—we are a global society—yet I still know people who regard half the world as mud brown. Some of their maps only have two colors on them: theirs and everyone else's. When I talk to the "everyone else" on school field trips, I learn that Christian evangelism has done more to dim their view of Christianity than anything else they know about it.

"Let us think of the bulk of your people who preach the gospel," Gandhi once said to an Indian missionary. "Do they spread the perfume of their lives? That is to me the sole criterion. All I want them to do is to live Christian lives, not to annotate them."[2]

As a convert myself, I get that. I endured torrents of words, landslides of words, ambulances and fire trucks full of words from earnest Christians eager to save me in high school and college. Some of them came after me like safari hunters after big game, others like census takers eager to make sure everyone was counted. All in all, their pursuit of me did not seem to have much to do with me. They were fulfilling a spiritual need of their own, as Pearl Buck said. The moment after I accepted Jesus as my Savior, they were gone.

In retrospect, the deeper problem was that they did not spread the perfume of their lives. There was nothing about them that made me want to be like them, at least not for very long. The people who eventually drew me to Christ never said a word about it—like my Methodist college adviser, whose unsentimental commitment to the welfare of his students lit my path to graduate school, or the Catholic priest who invited me into his kitchen to help cook spaghetti for the hungry hippies who would drop by later, or the Episcopal professor of New Testament who showed me what it looked like to love God with his whole heart *and* his considerable mind. None of them ever spoke to me about becoming Christian. I made that decision on my own, once I had been attracted by the fragrance of their faith.

Gandhi had a lot to say about Indian missionaries, who not only annotated a kind of life they did not live, but who also dangled medicine, education, and financial aid from their gospel sticks. If the lower-caste people to whom the missionaries reached out wanted any part of what was being offered to them, they had to take it all, including the Western cultural values that held the carrot in place. When Gandhi got his own chance to evangelize, he was quite brief.

"What would be your message to a Christian like me and my fellows?" an interviewer asked him once, to which Gandhi replied, "Become worthy of the message that is imbedded in the Sermon on the Mount, and join the spinning brigade."[3]

This goes on the long string of pearls given to me by people of other faiths, who can sometimes see mine more clearly than those of us on the inside can. In a single sentence, Gandhi has given me a new way to live with the verse at the end of Matthew's Gospel, which Christians sometimes call the Great Commission. The way to make a disciple is to be one. If your life does not speak, your footnotes will have limited impact. Become worthy of the message, and join the spinning brigade. Why isn't *that* the Great Commission?

There are many other ways that teaching Christianity has changed my practice of Christianity, but the one that has taken me farthest from the center of my tribe is the conviction that Christians do not have sole custody of the only way to God. I am willing to accept that Jesus is the only way for Christians. I am unwilling to accept that Christians get to decide he is the only

way for everyone else too. According to the King James Version
of the Bible, Jesus said, "I am the way, the truth, and the life: no
man cometh unto the Father but by me" (John 14:6). As Huston
Smith once said, everything hinges on what you think he meant
when he said "I."

He was sitting around the Last Supper table when he said
it, and I am pretty sure the subject was not interfaith relations.
The subject was Jesus's imminent arrest, his almost certain
death, and the real possibility that the people sitting around
the table with him would be the next to die, because they had
chosen his way, his truth, and his life. To my ear, at least, he
is reassuring them that they have made the right choice. He is
the only way for them. His truth is the one they have bet their
lives on, and he wants them to know that it leads straight to
the Father. There is no other way for them now. This is the only
way of life.

Even if this interpretation does not move you, perhaps we can
agree that Jesus's saying puts him in charge of deciding who is
on his way and who is not. If there is no other way to God, there
is no other gatekeeper. Jesus alone is the arbiter of salvation in
his name.

The New Testament scholar Amy-Jill Levine has told a particular story so often that I can hardly get it wrong, but you need
to know that she is Jewish in order to appreciate it. Here is how
it goes. When someone asks her for her interpretation of John
14:6, she says that she imagines herself at the pearly gates after a
long and happy life. While she is waiting in line with everyone
else to see whether St. Peter will let her into heaven, she makes
a list of everything she wanted to ask him while she was still in
the classroom. "Can you speak Greek? Where did you go when

you wandered off in the middle of Acts? What happened to your wife?"[4]

When it is finally her turn to talk to Peter, she starts pelting him with so many questions that he just waves her through. This concerns the next person in line, who has heard of Dr. Levine and knows she is a Jew. "Excuse me," the guy says to St. Peter, "but I don't think she's supposed to be here." That is when Jesus sticks his head through the gates and says, "It's fine, Peter. I know her, and she's okay by me." *Get it?* "No one comes to the Father but by me, and she's okay by me." Levine's point is that no one enters the presence of God except by God's grace. No church, no church doctrine, no individual gets to referee that. Where the Way of Jesus is concerned, he is the Decider.

None of this comes up in class. These are my bones to chew, not my students'. I do wonder how many of them are doing the same thing I am—trying to reconcile the Christian teachings they have received with their lives in a changing world. It is hard to hold your Christian identity in one hand and your complex sense of belonging in the other. As I said earlier, this is one of the reasons why more and more young people identify as spiritual but not religious. It is easier than trying to bridge the gap.

According to a recent poll by the Pew Research Center, the fastest growing religious group in the United States is the "nones"—the people who mark "none" on the survey question that asks for their religious affiliation. In 2014, there were almost 56 million of them, roughly 23 percent of the adult population. Ask me why, and I will tell you to go talk to your favorite person under thirty—but only if you are prepared to listen more than you talk. When I ask my favorite teenager to tell me about the chapel services at her Christian school, the conversation goes something like this:

"What do you call that thing when the person stands up and talks?" she asks me.

"A sermon?" I say.

"Yes," she says. "Someone told me you are good at it, but I don't know how it could possibly be good. There are two women who do it at my school, but no matter what they say they always end up with, 'And that's why you should believe in God.' It is so boring. There's a man too, but he's always talking about weddings. I feel like he has family issues or something."

"Have you ever heard anyone who wasn't boring?"

"There's one chaplain who doesn't get to do it much, but she's not boring. She tells stories about things that have really happened to her. She also has this thing she calls the wisdom stick. Sometimes she picks people out of the audience and taps them on the shoulder with it, like King Arthur with the knights. Then she asks them questions, and she always finds something good about their answers."

"How do her sermons end?"

"Let God guide you."

"Do you let God guide you?"

"God doesn't talk to me," she says. "I don't have that."

She is a teenager, but I know plenty of people older than she is who have the same problem. God does not talk to them either, at least not in the ways that they imagine God talking to other people. A few remember hearing God's voice when they were younger, which prompted some of them to join churches and others to step up their involvement in the ones to which they already belonged. This kept many of them busy for decades, but sooner or later they found themselves in the grips of what the writer Barbara Bradley Hagerty calls "mid-faith ennui."

"If you have striven to know God for a decade or more," she

writes, "you are almost certain to cross a spiritual wasteland, which ranges from dryness and boredom to agony and abandonment." Anyone who has read the classics of the Christian spiritual life recognizes this wilderness as a predictable stop on the journey into God. Augustine's *Confessions*, Teresa of Ávila's *Interior Castle*, and John of the Cross's *Dark Night of the Soul* all talk about it. As variously as people describe it, they all discover that if you are determined to walk the way of Jesus, there comes a time when you must leave the lower altitudes for the heights. This will involve lightening your pack and heading into parts unknown. You will have to leave your bags of spiritual sweets behind, along with the heavy devotional books you use to take your mind off how bad your feet hurt. Sooner or later you will have to leave all your soothing props behind, entrusting yourself to the God who cares more about your transformation than your comfort.

This lonely, heart-starving passage in the spiritual life is not any church's fault, but it is so downplayed by a majority of white Protestant churches—most of which survive by promoting the benefits of faith and not the costs—that spiritual ennui is "the crazy uncle of church life," Hagerty writes, "an embarrassment rarely mentioned in the company of believers."[5] When going to church makes you feel crazy and embarrassed, of course you stay home.

I understand the anxiety of mainline Christians who are watching congregations age and seminaries close, especially since I am one of them. It is hard to watch the wells from which you drew living water dry up. It is awful to watch people go away, leaving the dead to bury the dead—so awful that it is natural to try and find something else to blame. Blame the culture for shallowing the human mind. Blame the megachurches for peddling prosperity. Blame the world for leaving the church behind. There is some truth to all of these charges, which is why they generate so much energy. At the same time they obscure the last truth any of us wants to confront, which is that our mainline Christian lives are not particularly compelling these days. There is nothing about us that makes people want to know where we are getting our water. Our rose has lost its fragrance.

The students in my class may be failing Christianity, but Christianity is failing them too. If the Spirit is doing a new thing, I wish it would hurry up. Or maybe this *is* the new thing—a smaller, more humble version of church with less property and fewer clergy pensions; an odd collection of people meeting here and there as they try to figure out what it means to follow Jesus in a world of many faiths; a body with his name on it that is more willing than ever to let *him* decide who is with him and who is not.

This may be too much to ask. I like a soaring cathedral with a high pulpit and a huge pipe organ as much as the next person, but maybe it is time to swap that out for something that calls a little less attention to itself, something that frees up a little more energy for the neighbor. When everything else is gone, there is still that: the twinned love of God and neighbor, come to vivid life in the person of Jesus. Am I really meant to choose between him and my neighbors of other faiths?

I remember a night when it seemed as though I did. I was at a spirituality conference, sharing the stage with an orthodox Jewish artist. On Friday night the schedule included a Shabbat service led by a rabbi, followed by a Communion service led by a minister. The idea was that the one would flow into the other and that everyone would be welcome at both. The first part went fine. A Reconstructionist rabbi led the prayers in the auditorium where we were meeting. We thanked God for the week just past and for the opportunity to rest from it. At the end of the service the rabbi led us in some dancing and hand clapping that left us all breathless while a small crew transformed the bimah into a Communion table for what was coming next. I stood off to the side with the orthodox Jew, who made me painfully aware of what we were watching: the replacement of Jewish symbols with Christian ones as the rabbi left the room.

My companion began telling me how many members of his family had died in the Holocaust. He was named for one of them—an uncle—to keep the memory alive. He talked about what it was like for his generation to carry forward so much that had died or almost died in the concentration camps. He hoped I understood that he was not going to be able to take part in the Communion service. He would do his best to stay in the room, but what was about to happen cut so close to the pain of millions that it would not be easy for him.

Like every other Jew I knew, he was familiar with the verse near the end of Matthew's Gospel in which Pilate washes his hands at Jesus's trial, leaving Jesus's fate to his own people. According to Matthew, "the people as a whole answered, 'His blood be on us and on our children.'" With a verse like that ringing in your ears, I can see how a Communion cup full of Jesus's blood might drive you from the room.

I stayed with my companion while everyone else in the room circled around the Communion table. They were bathed in light. He and I stood twenty feet away in the dark at the edge of the circle. Listening to the familiar prayers from an unfamiliar distance, I wondered how they sounded to my new friend.

As our Savior Christ has taught us, we now pray.
O lamb of God.
This is my body, which is given for you.

Finally the celebrant broke the bread, and people started passing it around along with the wine. They all looked so joyous. My friend and I watched without speaking until someone noticed us and walked toward us with a cup of wine in one hand and a heel of bread in the other.

When she reached us and held them out, my friend shook his head and took a step back. Before I knew it, I had done the same thing. The Communion bearer walked away as quickly as she had come, leaving me to quiet the riot inside me. *What had I just done?* More important, why had I done it? I had refused the body and blood of Christ because it was painful to the person beside me. I had chosen to abstain with him rather than to participate without him. Though I knew full well that he did not expect that of me—that it was possible for a full-fledged Christian and a full-fledged Jew to stand together in their difference—at that moment I did not want to celebrate any Communion that did not include him.

I still do not know whether I failed Christianity that night or passed, but I did realize the truth of something I learned from Jonathan Sacks. "Peace involves a profound crisis of identity,"[6] he said. In my case, it also involved finding a new way to follow Jesus, even if that meant leaving the marked path.

Born Again

"Do not be astonished that I said to you, 'You must be born from above.' The wind blows where it chooses, and you hear the sound of it, but you do not know where it comes from or where it goes. So it is with everyone who is born of the Spirit." Nicodemus said to him, "How can these things be?" Jesus answered him, "Are you a teacher of Israel, and yet you do not understand these things?"

JOHN 3:7–10

The text I settled on for my baccalaureate address at the small university in upstate New York was John 3:1–15. After auditioning dozens of passages from Proverbs and Ecclesiastes that were full of universal wisdom, I decided to choose instead a piece of distinctly Christian wisdom. What better way to demonstrate that it was possible to speak from my own tradition without sounding triumphal or exclusive? At least I hoped I could do that, though it was up to my listeners to judge. Christians are not particularly gifted at knowing how we sound to others, especially in parts of the world where our voices are the loudest and most numerous.

The story of Jesus and Nicodemus appears only in John's Gospel. As traditionally told, it is a story about Nicodemus's inability to grasp the truth that Jesus reveals to him about the kingdom of God. Much is made of the fact that Nicodemus is a Pharisee, a Jew devoted to studying God's law and educating others in it. In Christian commentary, he is most often portrayed as the blind guide who cannot see what Jesus is holding out to him as plain as day.

I was drawn to his story for a couple of reasons. In the first place, I have always felt bad for Nicodemus. He comes to Jesus with questions that really matter to him, but he cannot understand a word that Jesus says. Jesus is hard on him too, the same way he was hard on the people in his hometown synagogue the first time he preached there. Meanwhile Nicodemus just sits there feeling stupid, trying over and over to make sense of Jesus's teaching before he falls silent in defeat. I feel bad for him because his silence is so often used against him, when it is a much more nimble response than trying to cover up his cluelessness with a lot of words. But the main reason I chose his story was because I thought it might have a hidden moral in it for young people under enormous pressure to prove how smart they were. "Are you a teacher of Israel, and yet you do not understand these things?"

With Piedmont students as my baseline, I predicted that the ones sitting in front of me at the baccalaureate would be vibrating with anxiety about the future. They had been trained to perform, to please, to excel, to succeed. For the past few months they had probably been asked ten times a day what they were going to do with their expensive education. Their parents were counting down the minutes until the flow of money would begin to reverse. Whatever the seniors' plans were, they were about to join the ranks of college graduates—a tiny percentage of the population of the planet—whose higher learning set them apart. They were the leaders of tomorrow, the people on whom the future depended, richly equipped to make the world a better place.

At least that was what the graduation speaker was going to tell them. The nice thing about being a baccalaureate preacher is that you do not have the last word. You have the next to last word, which is a good position for a subversive word—a spoken antidote to what is coming next in a person's life, or at least an analgesic. I thought it might help if I told the students that their old life was over, and that it was okay if they were clueless about the life to come. "You are about to enter a period of deep unknowing," I wanted to tell them, "which nothing you have learned will equip you to pass over. So relax if you can, because you are not doing anything wrong. This is what it means to be human."

There once was a Pharisee named Nicodemus, John says, who came to Jesus by night—presumably because he could ill afford to come by day, when everyone could see where he was going and ask him why. But it is also possible that Nicodemus came by night because he knew that was a better time to talk about things that matter. How often have you asked something by candlelight that you would never have asked under the light of a fluorescent bulb? Sometimes darkness is the perfect blanket for conversations you cannot have in the broad light of day.

Nicodemus leads with praise. "Rabbi," he says, "we know that you are a teacher who has come from God; for no one can do these signs that you do apart from the presence of God."

It has been a while since we pressed "Pause," but let me do it again. This story has evoked so much anti-Jewish teaching through the years that I do not have time to take it all apart right now, but if you happen to have received any of it, I hope you will be able to set it aside long enough to listen in on a very important conversation between two rabbis about the way of life.

As I said, Nicodemus leads with praise. The very first thing out of his mouth is an acknowledgment of Jesus's privileged relationship with God: "We know that you come from God." Why does Nicodemus say "we"? I do not know. Why does the Queen of England say, "We are very pleased to meet you" when she is all by herself? The point is, Nicodemus seems to be making an effort. He seems to be playing nice when Jesus all of a sudden delivers a karate chop.

"No one can see the kingdom of God without being born from above," Jesus says, but Nicodemus has not said a word about wanting to see the kingdom. Is Jesus slapping his opening compliment away? Or is he just putting an obstacle in front of the visiting rabbi to slow him down a little bit? That is what it sounds like to me. It sounds like Jesus is letting Nicodemus know that he does not know the first thing about who has come from God and who has not. Nicodemus may think he does, but he does not. He cannot see one millimeter into God's kingdom, because he has not been born from above. This conversation is deteriorating fast.

But Nicodemus does not take offense. He just keeps plowing ahead, running into more obstacles as he tries to make sense of what Jesus is saying. "How can anyone be born after having grown old?" he asks. "Can one enter a second time into the mother's womb and be born?" Poor Nicodemus is a literalist. He does not know that he is in John's Gospel, where nothing is ever (only) what it seems. Bread is not plain bread in this Gospel; it is the Bread of Life. Water is not plain water; it is Living Water that gushes up to Eternal Life. Every noun in this Gospel that has anything to do with Jesus is symbolically capitalized.

This birth Jesus is talking about, then, is not plain birth. It has nothing to do with talking your mother into letting you back in, so she can push you out again. The second time around, Jesus tells Nicodemus, the mother is the Spirit. Everyone who is born of her is made of her. No one enters the kingdom without this Birth. "Do not be astonished that I said to you, 'You must be born from above,'" Jesus says to Nicodemus, which is our best clue that even Jesus knows it is astonishing. "The wind blows where it chooses, and you hear the sound of it, but you do not know where it comes from or where it goes. So it is with everyone who is born of the Spirit."

At this point Nicodemus realizes he is in over his head. This teacher come from God has turned out to be a Zen teacher whose koans are impenetrable. Nicodemus came looking for clarity. He might have settled for cordiality, but what he has gotten instead is a brusque teaching that seems designed to keep him in the dark, where he feels really, really stupid.

"How can these things be?" Nicodemus says, and that is the last thing he says in this story. But the teacher who has rendered him mute is not through with him yet. Nicodemus has one more sunny prop that needs knocking out. "Are you a teacher of the people," Jesus asks him, "and yet you do not understand these things?" I hope he said that with irony, not meanness, but we will never know. All we know is that when Jesus finished talking, Nicodemus was gone—gone back through the dark to wherever he had come from, to take an Excedrin PM with a jigger of gin and try to get some sleep.

As many times as this story is told, Nicodemus is usually portrayed as the faithless skeptic—the guy who just did not get it—though there are Christian sixth graders who will shoot their hands in the air if you ask them what Jesus meant by being born again. "He meant that Nicodemus had to believe in him if he wanted to see the kingdom of God," one of them says. "He meant that once Nicodemus was baptized, the Spirit would come into him and he would understand everything. That's what Jesus was trying to tell him, but Nicodemus didn't have faith, so he didn't understand."

Maybe that is a useful function for the story—to help later Christians feel smarter than Nicodemus, more secure in our own beliefs, more sure of our own access to the divine. Plus, it matches the pedagogy that most of us know best. When the teacher asks you a question, you are supposed to give the right answer, for which you will get points, or strokes, or both—the explicit and implicit rewards of knowing the right answer. But what if Jesus is not that kind of teacher? What if his purpose is not to enlighten Nicodemus but to endarken him, establishing the limits of what humans can know about God and what we cannot?

"We know," Nicodemus says to Jesus when he first comes into the room.

"You do not know," Jesus says to Nicodemus right before he leaves.

If you interpret this as a judgment on Nicodemus, then the story is fairly straightforward. Nicodemus does not know things he ought to know. If he knew them, Jesus's meaning would be clear to him. His unknowing is his fatal flaw, the one that prevents him from being born again, which ends his conversation with Jesus and forces him back into the night from which he came. But that is not what the story says. If you take the buds out of your ears (the ones playing the old tape of what this story is supposed to mean) and listen carefully to what Jesus is saying, he is saying the exact opposite.

"The wind blows where it chooses," he says to Nicodemus, "and you hear the sound of it, but you do not know where it comes from or where it goes." This is not a judgment. It is a statement of fact, as you can tell from the very next thing Jesus says. "So it is with everyone who is born of the Spirit." *Everyone.* Nicodemus is not a special case. No one knows where the Spirit comes from or where it goes. *No one.* The only thing that sets Nicodemus apart is that he is so uncomfortable with his unknowing. His problem is that he thinks he *ought* to know.

This is a difficult teaching for those who want to feel secure in their relationship with God, especially if their security depends on knowing how things work. When and where is the Spirit present? Who has access to it and who does not? What does it mean to be born of the Spirit? What must one do to experience second birth? How can one be sure it has happened, and what are the consequences for those to whom it does not happen? Are they eligible for heaven or not?

"You do not know," Jesus says. Not because you are stupid, but because you are not God. So relax if you can, because you are not doing anything wrong. This is what it means to be human.

That is more or less what I told the students at their baccalaureate service. Whatever your grade point average, whatever your relationship to religion, whatever people tell you about how the sky is the limit and you can achieve anything you put your mind to, there is a place where human knowing runs out. Strong winds really do blow through people's lives, and the Spirit does not hand out maps showing where the wind came from, where it is going, how you are supposed to handle it, and how everything will turn out in the end. Only the Weather Channel does that.

The Spirit gives you life.

She comes and goes.

She is beyond your control.

Any questions?

I do not know how the sermon went over with the students, since I had no opportunity to talk with them afterward. They had lots of partying to do. The leaders of the Jewish and Muslim student organizations smiled at me when I sat down. The chaplain did not look stricken, which seemed like a good sign. As we all stood to sing the final hymn, the president of the college shared his hymnal with me. Since I knew he was Jewish, he startled me by singing harmony on every verse of the Christian hymn. When he registered my surprise, he leaned over and said, "I went to an Episcopal prep school. I know them all." Two hours later I was on the airplane home, writing the final exam for Religion 101.

Preachers learn early on that we preach the sermons we most need to hear, and that was true of the one I had just preached as well. The story of Jesus and Nicodemus freed me from believing I had to know the answer to every question about what it means to be Christian. Church disunity, disrespectful evangelism, exclusive truth claims, triumphal language—I would never stop chewing on those bones, but they would not bother me as much once I allowed that I could never know everything there was to know about them. I could also stop worrying about whether I was Christian enough to stay in the room with Jesus. Thanks to his conversation with Nicodemus, I gained new respect for what it means to be *agnostic*—such a maligned word, so often used to mean distrustful or lackadaisical, when all it really means is that *you do not know*, which according to Jesus is true of everyone who is born of the Spirit.

Thanks to Nicodemus, I started borrowing a line from Maya Angelou, recipient of the 2010 Presidential Medal of Freedom, who said she was always amazed when people came up to her and told her they were Christian. "I think, 'Already?'" she said. "'You already got it?'"

"I'm working at it," she continued, "which means that I try to be as kind and fair and generous and respectful and courteous to every human being."[1] She was in her eighties when she said that. It sounded like the perfect Christian baseline to me: how you treat every human being, neighbor and stranger alike. Even if you are still working at it, that is the mustard seed.

The greatest gift of my second birth, however, was being re-united with my birth mother—not the first one, who bore me in the labor and delivery suite at Lafayette Home Hospital in La-fayette, Indiana—but the second one, who bore me from above. Like plenty of other Christians, I had focused most of my devo-tion on Jesus through the years. Almost all of the prayers in my prayer book ended with "through Jesus Christ our Lord," so I was conditioned to turn toward him every time I said, "Amen." He was also the easiest Person of the Trinity to identify with. Even if I got the details wrong—height, weight, skin color, eyes—there was no question that God the Son looked human. He was put together like me. Well, almost like me.

God the Father, on the other hand, was the Big Invisible. In regal mode, He was the God of thunderheads and lightning bolts. In benign mode, He was the humming energy of the uni-verse, filling up all the empty space between human cells, quan-tum particles, and planets. When I was a child I imagined Him with a lot of white hair and a great bushy beard, most at home on a gold throne in the heavens. God the Father was a dead ringer for Zeus.

God the Holy Spirit was the hardest to visualize. How do you picture the wind? The biblical image of the dove seems to have

captured the artistic imagination. In one medieval painting after another, a downward facing dove holds steady over the crown
of thorns on Jesus's head while God the Father leans out a window of clouds even higher up. A falconer might be forgiven for
thinking the dove looks more like a hawk dropping on its prey.
This dangerous idea is repeated in depictions of the Spirit as a
flame of fire, licking up the side of a wooden cross. It does not
look dangerous in the logo of the United Methodist Church, but
I think that is an illusion. Once the wind of God and the fire of
God get together, the dove of God had better climb to a higher
altitude. The Spirit is the least predictable Person of the Trinity,
the one most likely to slip the leash and save in unorthodox ways.
Just listen to the way Jesus defends her freedom to Nicodemus.

Her. For reasons beyond my understanding, this simple
change of pronouns solves all my problems with God the Spirit.
If I am born of her, she is my mother. If I am not born of her,
she may yet return for me. No one knows when she may come
blowing through the trees, the windows, the open doors, pitch-
ing all the papers off the desk and making the houseplants shiver
in their pots. As scary as she may sometimes be, I can let her
blow me around. When she flings me into other people, she is
trying to tell me something. When she drops me off in unfamiliar places, I need to pay attention. She is completely trustwor-
thy, even when I cannot explain a single thing she is up to. She
comes. She goes. She gives life to all creation. I have plenty more
questions, but the answers are not vital as long as God the Spirit
keeps breathing on me.

Once I started reading up on the third Person of the Trinity, I discovered how many theologians were ahead of me.[2] The
feminine pronoun is not as important to all of them as it is to
me, but the idea of divine multiplicity is—the idea that one God

can answer to more than one name and assume more than one form. Even if Christians will not go higher than three, the case is made: unity expresses itself in diversity. The One who comes to us in more than one way is free to surprise us in all kinds of ways. This is especially meaningful to people like me, who mean to hang on to our singular Christian identity with one hand and our love of many neighbors with the other. Within the community of the Trinity, the one and the many do not cancel each other out. They lean toward one another in eternally circling, mutually inclusive love. That is the image in which the rest of us are made.

I will never figure this out, but that is *good* news, not bad. To walk the way of sacred unknowing is to remember that our best ways of thinking and speaking about God are provisional. They are always in process—reflecting our limited perspectives, responding to our particular lives and times, relating us to our ancestors in the faith even as they flow out toward the God who remains free to act in ways that confound us. If our ways of thinking and speaking of God are not at least that fluid, then they are not really theologies but *theolatries*—things we worship instead of God, because we cannot get God to hold still long enough to pin God down.

Lately I have begun to notice how my holy envy of friends in other traditions moves around the circle back to me. An observant Jewish friend tells me that he envies my ability to eat anything with anyone. He is committed to eating kosher, but sometimes it gets in his way. He watches the omnivorous Christians at the interfaith banquet and wonders what that must be like. A Buddhist says that she envies the devotion Christians show for Mary and her child. There are a few stories that feature the Buddha as a child, she says, but since his mother died a week after he was born there is nothing to compare with the tender relationship between Mary and her baby.

On my next visit to the Vedanta Center of Atlanta, the Hindu swami welcomes the students by offering an impromptu homily on the Collect for Purity—a jewel in the crown of the Episcopal prayer book. I have no idea how he came to know it by heart, but his talk includes quotes from the prophet Isaiah and the Sermon on the Mount as well. Listening to him speak so reverently of my sacred scriptures, I realize that I cannot recite a single verse of his. By the time he has finished, I am more aware than ever of the perfect love made manifest in Jesus—and all thanks to my friend the swami.

On another occasion, I join two Christian friends and their Muslim colleague for lunch at the school where they all teach religion. When the Muslim woman does not order lunch, I offer her some of mine. She reminds me that it is Ramadan and says she will catch up after the sun goes down. Then we get into a conversation about the trouble in Israel/Palestine.

"At this point I think it is up to you," she says, looking around the table.

"Us?" I say.

"You Christians," she says. "You are the peacemakers, are you not? Perhaps you can see a way through where others cannot." Clearly she does not know the same Christians I do. Or maybe it is a full-blown case of holy envy from her side, in which the neighbor's yard looks greener than her own. Either way, her view of my tradition is so much more positive than mine that I sit up straighter.

Later, listening to a famous atheist being interviewed on National Public Radio, I am intrigued when the host asks him about atheist humanitarian movements. In hot spots all around the world, the host says, Christians show up with medical supplies, doctors, bottled water, food, and tents, often at great risk to themselves. Muslims do too. Are there any atheist efforts to compare with that, he asks his guest? The atheist cannot think of any at the moment. All of a sudden I see my crowd differently— even the ones who irk me by handing out Bibles with their aid. They are there, and I am not, which tells you everything you need to know about who is irking God the most.

In these and other ways I learn positive things about my tradition from people who do not belong to it, which triples the value of their praise. Without knowing it, they have joined the throng of my Melchizedeks—the perfect strangers who arrive with blessings on my tribe and go back to their own rejoicing. When I consider their gifts to me, I decide that part of being born again is looking for ways to return the favor, like the imam who sent my students away with the express wish that they be the best Christians, the best Jews, the best human beings they could be. Once you have given up knowing who is right, it is easy to see neighbors everywhere you look.

As far as I can tell, the only thing Nicodemus did wrong on the night he met with Jesus was to leave the room. If he had only been able to stay put with the sting of his ignorance a little longer—the fear of losing his grip, the anxiety of his unanswerable questions—if only he had been able to forgive himself, then a whole new way of life might have opened up for him. You should know by now that I am not suggesting he might have become a Christian—that is the old tape playing—but he might have found a new way to be a leader of the people that did not require him to be omniscient.

Divine Diversity

In my Father's house there are many dwelling places.
If it were not so, would I have told you that I go to
prepare a place for you?

JESUS OF NAZARETH

One of the greatest gifts that holy envy has given me is the ability to reimagine my own tradition. I would like to tell you that it is the product of gaining wisdom, insight, and perspective through the study of other religions, but that would not be true. Instead, it is the product of losing my way, doubting my convictions, interrogating my religious language, and tossing many of my favorite accessories overboard when the air started leaking out of my theological life raft. Only then was I scared and disoriented enough to see something new when I looked back at my old landmarks, many of which I was approaching from an unfamiliar angle.

I do not know if this has ever happened to you, but once, a long time ago, I lost a dog. She was only ten months old—my first Jack Russell terrier. She was wearing a new collar, so when she smelled something exciting on the wind just before sunset, she slipped her leash before I even felt her tug. Then she was

gone, with more than a hundred acres to explore, while I ran
behind her calling her name as though she cared. I chased her
through brush, through running streams, and through barbed
wire fences before she finally paused for breath and I grabbed
her by the tail that had been cropped for exactly that purpose.
Then she panted happily in my arms while I tried to remember
where my house had gone.

About twenty minutes later I walked up a hill toward a barn,
trying to figure out whether I had arrived at the Tiptons' place
or the Holcombs'. The barn was weathered, like the Tiptons', but
it was also unpainted, like the Holcombs'. Then I realized it was
my own barn I was looking at, though from such an unfamiliar
angle that it was as if I had never seen it before. I was also extremely stressed, which meant that I was much more invested in
the dog in my arms than the barn on the hill. Either way, I was
totally charmed when my own barn snapped into view, and I saw
it as if for the first time. Should this ever happen to you—with
a barn, a person, a photograph, or a religious truth—please do
not overlook the gift. It is a great thing to see something familiar
from an unfamiliar angle for the first time, even if it is because
you have been worried and lost for longer than you would have
liked.

After I saw the Nicodemus story from an unfamiliar angle for
the first time, I was wide open to being surprised by new views of
other familiar stories as well. This reminded me of something Jonathan Sacks had taught me back at the beginning of my journey—
about how important it is for people of faith to make space for
difference at the heart of our tradition. Common human values
are great, he said, but when our groupishness sets in and we are
looking for excuses to wipe each other out, we need stories from
deep within our own tradition that show us another way. This is

especially important for monotheists, he said, whose focus on one God can so easily lead us to believe we are the only apple of God's eye. What we need instead are new understandings—each of us based on our own scriptures and traditions—that the unity of the Creator is expressed in the diversity of creation.

By this time it had become clear to me that human diversity transcends the diversity of religions. People of faith also need help living with people who reject faith along with people of uncertain faith, who come in a wide mix of colors, classes, cultures, politics, genders, means, and abilities. Any one of these differences has as much or more power to divide people than religion, which assigns religions the additional task of making room for difference as well as conferring blessings on their own followers. Fortunately, this is something that the great religions all have in common. Whether they confess faith in the same creator-God, they agree that the truth of their teaching hinges on how people treat one another: with partiality or justice, with dishonor or dignity, with cruelty or compassion.

When I began reimagining my tradition, I went back as far as I could—in my case, to the story of the Tower of Babel, which occurs early in the book of Genesis. According to the storyteller, everyone in the world spoke the same language at that point. They all used the same words, which made it easy for them to agree to build a city so grand that the top of its tower reached the heavens. They did this without checking with God first, and when God discovered what they were up to, God was not pleased. According to the book of Genesis:

> The LORD came down to see the city and the tower, which mortals had built. And the LORD said, "Look, they are one people, and they have all one language; and this is only the

beginning of what they will do; nothing that they propose
to do will now be impossible for them. Come, let us go
down, and confuse their language there, so that they will
not understand one another's speech." (11:5–7)

After that the people could not understand each other anymore. When they tried to talk, it sounded like babble. They got
absolutely nowhere. With their unity in tatters, they left their
half-built city where it stood and went away in different directions with anyone who could understand what they were saying. From that point forward, the story of humanity became the
story of divided tribes and nations who had lost the ability to
understand each other—and all because they disobeyed God.

That is how the story is usually told anyway. As with the story
of Nicodemus, it is not what the Bible says, but for those who are
not paying close attention it does seem to suggest that God's original plan was for humans to be the same. Then we screwed things
up, and God made us different to slow our malfeasance down.

For those who regard the New Testament as sacred scripture,
the curse of Babel is reversed soon after Jesus's resurrection,
when in Acts 2 the Holy Spirit sweeps through a house in Jerusalem and gives the disciples the gift of tongues. They start speaking languages they never learned in school, so that people from
all over the world are able to understand what they are saying.
The damage done at Babel is undone by the power of the Holy
Spirit—but only for a single morning. Once the disciples have
settled down and their flames have gone back to the pilot light,
they face the same challenges everyone else does: making themselves understood to people who do not speak their language.
Like it or not, human diversity is here to stay. All that remains to
be seen is how we will deal with it.

Emmanuel Lartey was the first person to reveal the counternarrative in the story of Babel to me. I saw his name in the program of a big religion conference where he was scheduled to speak about "polydoxy," a word that was not in my vocabulary then and is not in my dictionary now. Lartey is a distinguished professor of pastoral theology who was raised in Ghana, which helps explain why he used the lens of colonialism to retell the story of Babel. That was the hill he climbed to see the story anew.

The way he reimagined the story of Babel, it was not about God's judgment on diversity but God's judgment on the dominance of one people, with one language, whose wish to make a name for themselves took over their lives. God saved them by confusing their language, so they could not complete their domination project. God defused their hegemony and scattered them like hot ashes, so their ambitious fire would not spread. In this telling, the moral of the story is that God favors the diversity of many peoples over the dominance of any one people. I could not write down what Professor Lartey was saying fast enough to keep up, so I hope if he ever reads this, he says, "Close enough."

His reimagining of the Babel story reminded me of Jewish midrash—a tradition I greatly envy—in which Jews both ancient and modern respond to contemporary problems by creating new stories based on close readings of the Bible. The first midrash I found about Babel was all about bricks. In this old story, the tower of Babel grew and grew until it took a full year for people to pass the bricks from hand to hand all the way to the top. Bricks became so precious to the project that when a brick slipped and fell, the people wept, but when a human being fell and died, no one paid any attention.[1]

Another old story says that building the tower became more important than anything else including giving birth. When a pregnant woman felt her labor pains begin, she was not allowed to stop making bricks. Instead, she "brought forth while she was making bricks, carried her child in her apron, and continued to make bricks."[2] These legends are not in the Bible, which never says exactly what went wrong in Babel. Was it that people had let bricks become more important to them than each other? Was it that they huddled together in one place instead of being fruitful and filling the earth as God had commanded them? Was it their abandonment of agrarian life for urbanization? The Bible never says.

In my interpretation, it does not really matter what went wrong. Human beings are so capable of all the possibilities— overreaching, underreaching, and everything in between—that it hardly matters which one you decide to blame. The most interesting part of the story is the ending anyway, with the cascade of new tongues that signaled a change in God's plans. Once God saw how things were working out for the people who spoke the same language, God revised God's will. God tweaked the humans, so they were as various as all the other creatures God had made. From that point forward, the languages of three people would be as different as the songs of three birds. Wouldn't that be an improvement over a world in which all birds sounded alike?

For reasons no one may ever understand, God decided it would be helpful for people to be different instead of the same, if only because it would slow them down a little bit. God decided it would be *good* for them to have to stop on a regular basis and say, "Could you say that a different way, please? I don't understand what you mean" or "Can you show me with your hands?" God decided it would be *good* for them to stop taking their communication for granted and work a little harder at trying to understand each other.

One of the first things they understood (in my midrash, at least) was that there was more than one way to say something important. *Hashem. Brahman. Sunyata. Holy Trinity. Allah.* Sometimes, when they used words like these, they were pointing at the same thing, and sometimes they were not, but just trying to explain the words slowed them down long enough to make them think about what they really meant. *What do you mean when you say God?* This was not a problem they had when they all understood each other. They had just assumed that they meant the same thing when they used the same word, which was not the case at all—but speaking the same language had allowed them to cling to that illusion for longer than was good for them. Then God came to their rescue and confused their speech.

Translation became a necessary human activity. When there was not an equivalent word for something in another language, people had to settle for second best, which was how they came to understand the importance of charity as well as precision. When they could not say exactly what they meant, they let the frustration of that soften them toward other people who could not say exactly what they meant either.

Eventually those who spoke Finnish had a word for a large herd of reindeer that did not exist in Japanese. Those who spoke Japanese had a word for sunlight that filters through trees that did not exist in Rukwangali. Those who spoke Rukwangali had a word for tiptoeing across warm sand that did not exist in Finnish. Eventually people began to understand that not everything could be said in words. Some things were better expressed with a lifted eyebrow, a tilted head, a hand reaching out to put something in another hand. *What do you mean when you say human?*

You see where I am going with this. By revising the divine will and creating a world full of people who spoke different languages, God chose variety over uniformity. God created the conditions for multiple interpretations of everything that required speech to describe. There was no longer one right way to say a true thing. There were many ways to say it. *Torah. Veda. Dharma. Gospel. Qur'an.* Even when those words pointed to different things, you could see how much they meant to the people who said them.

But trying to figure out *how* they were different proved so frustrating to some people that they decided to settle down with people who spoke the same language they did. Just because God had changed God's mind did not mean they had to change theirs. They settled in places where they would not have to learn anyone else's language, and they resented it when people who did not speak their language moved in next door. Others took up the challenge of becoming multilingual, gaining new neighbors every time they learned to say, "Good morning!" in a different language.

"The greatest single antidote to violence is *conversation*," says Jonathan Sacks, "speaking our fears, listening to the fears of others, and in that sharing of vulnerabilities discovering a genesis of hope."[3] The vulnerabilities cannot be undersold. Sometimes they are so great that they make my teeth chatter. When I listen to someone describe reality in a foreign language that nonetheless makes enormous sense to me, my own hold on reality is shaken. When I try to describe what I believe to be true to someone who does not believe it, my certainty springs alarming leaks. I am lost in the woods trying to find the life that makes meaning out of mine.

There are plenty of times I want to go back to Babel, where

everyone speaks my language and we are all on the same page. My own church feels that way sometimes, like a safe city with a tower that has a cross on top, making a name for its builders by how far it reaches into the heavens. It is a beautiful place to rest, but it is not the best place to stay. If God's revised will for Babel is any indication, then the clamorous world outside is the best place for human beings to stay—to stay on the move, that is, entering into conversations with neighbors who are as different from one another as they can be. In the United States plenty of them are farther from their safe places than I will ever be, which makes my efforts to communicate with them all the more important.

Why do it at all, when the chances of agreeing on politics, religion, or anything else are so slim? I cannot answer that question for anyone else. My sole hope is to give God one more chance to work on me, by coming to me in the guise of a stranger who does not speak my language, asking me questions I cannot answer, until I become so interested in what can and cannot be said that the stranger and I go off to find lunch, leaving our half-built tower standing silent in the sand.

Way back at the beginning of this book, I said that one of the reasons I left parish ministry for the classroom was because the living water in my well was running low. My bucket kept hitting sand. My cup did not overflow. I moved to the classroom in order to learn more about what was in other people's sacred wells and how they served it up. Though I had faith even then that all our water came from the same sacred source, I did not think that was something I could say in church. Our Christian sediment had settled pretty definitively by then. No one seemed very interested in shaking it up, and even I could see why.

There were kids in my church. There were new people who

were just coming to faith. They needed to learn the Christian story before they started reimagining the story. They needed to tend their own holy ground before they began seeing how the yard next door might be holy too. Envy could wait—but should it ever arise in them, I want them to know that it does not mean there is something wrong with them. It just means they are ready to meet some new neighbors. By God's grace, it means they are ready to draw the circle wider.

Laurie Patton, the president of Middlebury College, once asked me a question that I have never been able to forget. "What is the story you are working on," she asked, "that doesn't have an ending yet?" In the years since she first asked that question I have come up with many different answers, but today my answer is: the story I have told so far in this book. After becoming so disillusioned with my faith that I could not look it in the eyes, I have left as many of its self-interested truth claims as I can, arriving at a place where it is possible to resume the work of loving God and my neighbor as self-forgetfully as possible. This is more than enough Christian teaching for a lifetime. It seems unlikely that I will ever get around to selling all my possessions or forgiving anyone seventy-seven times. Most days I cannot even bridle my tongue. But I can love more. I know that. I also know how much it can cost, which is why I do not do it more often.

While I am waiting to learn how this story I am working on ends, I will continue to ask much of my tradition, especially since it has much to answer for. I will keep insisting that it produce good fruit in a changing world, even as it helps me and others like me catch the new wine of the Spirit that is being poured out. When I am thirsty, I will dip my cup in the well nearest to hand, while longing to return home to the one I know best. Even if the water in the Christian well does not belong to Christians—even if it is funded by the same great underground river that feeds all other wells—I know where mine is and I know how to use it. My Christian cup works well enough, and when it does not, I can still use my hands.

The God You Didn't Make Up

The Spirit arrives incognito, bringing the indwelling
love of God. Those who do not refuse it become lovers
of the only God there is, because the only God there
is has loved them first.

CHARLES HEFLING

A few years into my tenure at Piedmont College I was invited
to teach Christian spirituality at a Presbyterian seminary
during the summer term. The baccalaureate address was behind
me, which meant that I was comfortable on the sacred way of
unknowing—so comfortable, in fact, that I was not sure I knew
what "spirituality" meant anymore. Maybe no one was. Maybe
"spirituality" was another of those words we use without thinking very much about what we mean. So I started asking people
what they meant by it, building a list of definitions that included
everything from "Spirituality is an escape hatch for people who
would rather live in heaven than on earth" to "Spirituality is
anything that helps you feel closer to God."

Finally I asked my friend Judy, who spent many years as a
student of Sufism and who embodies *fana*—the self-annihilating
love of God—as well as anyone I know. When I asked her to

define spirituality for me, she thought for a moment and said, "Spirituality is the active pursuit of the God you didn't make up." I loved that. I also did not know what it meant.

I could not argue with the part about making God up. All you have to do is dust my Bible for fingerprints to find the favorite parts and the ignored ones—or follow my tracks on Google, or check my book purchases on Amazon, or poll my friends. I stick very close to sources that support my view of reality. Even when that view shifts, as it does every time I teach Religion 101, I still gravitate toward the new truths that sound the most like mine. There is really no easy entry for anyone with whom I seriously disagree about who God is and how God does (or does not) act.

Through the years I have worked hard on my divine mosaic, which reflects my hopes and fears about God all the way from my early childhood until now. It has pieces in it that I collected from the various churches I have passed through, from classes I have taught and taken, from my favorite teachers and writers about God. It has more than I like to admit from my social location in this world—a rich white woman who has never so much as broken a bone—and from my North American-ness, in which I am so immersed that it is invisible to me except when someone points it out.

Once, when I wrote an article for *The Christian Century* about the fortunate alignment of Easter with the spring equinox (so that the grass really is "springing green" when Resurrection Sunday arrives in Georgia), the editor received at least two angry letters from readers in New Zealand and Australia, where Easter arrives in autumn, following their spring equinox in September. What can I say? I never saw it that way. It was one more of those things I needed someone else to point out to me.

None of this makes my mosaic bad or wrong. It simply confirms that I made it up. *How rude of Judy to point that out.* My view of God is my own creation, made from bits and pieces of received or perceived knowledge about divine reality that I hope or fear are true. My mosaic has my fingerprints all over it. Ask anyone what she means when she says "God" and chances are that you will learn a lot more about that person than you will learn about God. So how does one get beyond that? How do any of us actively pursue the God we did not make up?

For a number of years I thought I had to surpass Christian tradition to get there, rising above all the familiar words and images in order to open myself to the divine reality that lay far beyond them all. The more I learned about the religions of the world, the more I became convinced that they were all pointing to the same sacred mystery beyond all human understanding, so why not stop granting priority to any religious language and become more proficient in them all?

Some of my farsighted friends had already gone there, devoting themselves to the perennial wisdom that funds all of the world's great religions without granting priority to any of them. Following their lead, I learned as many faith languages as I could, gaining a great deal from the distinctions Hindus make between the God who is made manifest in physical form (think *Jesus*) and the God who transcends form (think *Spirit*). I gained similar insights from learning about the differences between Theravada Buddhists (who emphasize liberating the self) and Mahayana Buddhists (who emphasize liberating others), which helped me think differently about Christians who emphasize individual salvation and those who emphasize social justice.

I could go on. There is no way to overstate the importance of what I have learned from studying the world's great religions, but here is what I noticed: I was still drawn to the teachings that

I liked. I did not spend much time on the hot and cold hells of Buddhism, for instance, which include being impaled on a fiery spear until flames come out the nose and mouth, and being frozen until one's body cracks open and internal organs are exposed. It was easy to think of Christian parallels, but I did not want to go there. Neither was I drawn to learn more about the antipathy some Muslims have toward dogs or the Native American ceremony that involves eating sacred puppy stew. But this is not about what other people do; this is about what I do: I make my own mosaic. Whether the resources at my disposal come only from my own tradition or from a wide array of traditions, my ego stays very active selecting the ones that please me most. So how is this any different from the gospel cherry-picking that drives me crazy when I see members of my own religion doing it?

There is an additional problem, which is that I am not a born multilinguist. As hard as I work at learning other religious languages, the subtle differences between the subdenominations of Shia Muslims are as difficult for me to understand as the differences between the Christian Church (Disciples of Christ), the Churches of Christ, and the unaffiliated Christian churches and churches of Christ, all of which grew from the American Restoration Movement of the early nineteenth century. If the way forward involves panoramic knowledge of other faiths, then I do not see how someone like me is ever going to get there. I am barely up to speed on the historical record of my own denomination, which is only a couple of hundred years old.

I had a kind of epiphany during the spring semester, in the middle of an upper-level course on death and dying in the world's great religions. After the students and I had learned the main differences in the ways Hindus, Buddhists, Jews,

Muslims, and Christians treat their dying and lay their dead to rest, we learned about the vast differences *within* those traditions, depending on everything from cultural background to theological worldview. Catholics and Protestants do not do things the same way any more than Sunni and Shia Muslims do. Hindus who live in India do things differently from Hindus who live in Great Britain. American converts to Buddhism are worlds apart from Asian Americans who received the tradition from their parents and grandparents. How was I ever going to learn all of that?

Imagine being a hospital chaplain in a major urban center. Your first visit of the day takes you to the room of an Orthodox Jew who is having a small refrigerator installed in his room for ready-to-eat kosher food during his stay. He asks you to make sure to call *his* rabbi, not a Reform rabbi, to come to see him. From there you go to the room of an elderly Hindu woman who is clearly dying and whose family is trying to lift her out of bed to put her on a blanket on the floor according to their custom. After you have alerted the nursing staff to that eventuality, you head to the room of a Sikh child on the pediatric oncology floor, where the child's mother is trying to explain to the lab tech why the child's steel bracelet—the symbol of a Sikh's unbreakable bond with God—is not coming off even if it does get in the way of the IV tubing.

While I was getting hand cramps from writing all of this down, I came upon these two sentences in the assigned reading:

It may help immensely to have competence in the language of the bereaved person and to know much about that person's culture, but often what is most helpful is to be authentically human. At times, a genuine and caring offer of sympathy, shared tears, or a hug has more meaning than stilted efforts to try to act like people in the other person's culture.[1]

"But often what is most helpful is to be authentically human." I highlighted that. When I got to class the next day, I found that most of the students had highlighted it too, so we spent the rest of the hour talking about what it means to be authentically human. It was a lot like trying to define spirituality, or God.

"I think empathy is key," one young man said. "You have to be able to imagine yourself in another person's place, no matter how different they are from you."

"I think it has more to do with touching people than talking to them," said a young woman who had spent a lot of time as a hospital patient herself.

"I think you have to ask permission first," a third person said. "What's comforting to you might not be comforting to someone else."

We went on for a full hour this way, which gave me plenty of time to notice how many kinds of human beings were sitting around the table. There were only seven of them, but they included majors in mass communication, criminal justice, history, nursing, and psychology as well as philosophy and religion. They had roots in Vietnam, Puerto Rico, Mexico, the United States, and Brazil. The youngest was in her twenties, the oldest in her forties. One was a military veteran. One was a mother. Two were in Twelve Step programs, which they referenced frequently. Three more were Catholics. They all identified as Christian, though their beliefs covered the gamut and often canceled each other out. I could not have asked for a better panel of experts on what it means to be authentically human.

We did not try to reach full consensus. We knew each other too well for that, but we also knew each other well enough to allow for differences—sometimes significant ones—in how we viewed ultimate matters of life and death. When someone said he wanted his ashes to be tucked in the ground around the seed of a great tree, the person who wanted a full funeral with a wooden casket nodded. When someone said she did not want to be embalmed, someone else remembered how pretty her grandmother had looked after the undertaker had gotten done with her. Maybe you had to be there, but it seemed to me that the way we were talking and listening to each other said volumes about what it means to be authentically human. Even if we never reached agreement about the things that mattered most, we could still lean toward each other instead of away.

That was the day I decided to make peace with my own religious language, for at least two reasons. In the first place, no one can speak all the religious languages in the world, and there is no spiritual Esperanto. None of us can speak "language." We have to speak *a* language before we can learn anyone else's, and the carefulness with which we speak our own can make us better listeners to others. In the second place, my religious language is quite excellent at speaking of what it means to be authentically human.

In Christian terms, it means being made in the image of God—not just you, but everyone. It means tending the neighbor's welfare as religiously as you tend your own. It means letting the splinter you see in the other person's eye alert you to the log in your own. It means opening the door to the soldiers when they come, so your friends can get away. It means crossing all kinds of boundaries to meet people where they are and arguing with people on your own side who want to call you out for that. It even means "losing it" from time to time, because being authentically human can be so effing exhausting, especially with people who want you to be God. Who knows that better than Jesus?

In my religious language, there is no loving God without loving other human beings—or, as a disciple named John said more forcefully in one of his letters, "Those who do not love a brother or sister whom they *have* seen, cannot love God whom they have *not* seen." You will have your own interpretation of this teaching and others like it, but here is what they reveal to me: the same God who came to the world in the body of Jesus comes to me now in the bodies of my neighbors, because God knows that a body needs a body to make things real, and the real physical presence of my neighbors makes them much harder for me to romanticize, fantasize, demonize, or ignore than any of the ideas I have of them in my head.

If I could make my neighbors up, I could love them in a minute. I could make them in my own image, looking back at me with deep gratitude for how *authentically human* I am being to them—and they to me!—reading poetry to each other, admiring pictures of each other's grandchildren, and taking casseroles to each other when we are sick. But nine times out of ten these are not the neighbors I get. Instead, I get neighbors who cancel my vote, burn trash in their yard, and shoot guns so close to my house that I have to wear an orange vest when I walk to the mailbox. These neighbors I did not make up knock on my front door to offer me the latest issue of *The Watchtower*. They put things on their church signs that make me embarrassed for all Christians everywhere. They text while they drive, flipping me off when I pass their expensive pickup trucks on the right, in spite of the fish symbols on their shiny rear bumpers.

But if you stop and think about it, what better way could there be for me to actively pursue the God I did not make up—the one I cannot see—than to try for even twelve seconds to love these brothers and sisters whom I *can* see? What better way to shatter my custom-made divine mosaic than to accept that these fundamentally irritating and sometimes frightening people are also made in the image of God? Honest to goodness, with a gospel like that you could empty a church right out.

Yet this, in a nutshell, is the monumental spiritual challenge of living with religious difference—and more centrally than that—of living with anyone who does not happen to be me. "Love God in the person standing right in front of you," the Jesus of my understanding says, "or forget the whole thing, because if you cannot do that, then you are just going to keep making shit up."

It took my husband, Ed, and me years to make peace with that truth. I keep thinking he likes cities, but that is me, not him. He keeps thinking I like power tools, but that is him, not me. When he is hurt, he likes to be held. When I am hurt, I like to be left alone until the urge to bite someone passes. Now Ed and I operate by our first amendment to the Golden Rule, which is not "Do unto others as you would have them do unto you," but "Do unto others as *they* would have you do unto them (instead of thinking they are just like you)."

I know that my Jesus mosaic is as much my own creation as my God mosaic is, but when I follow him through the Gospels it seems like he is always pouring himself out in one direction or another—into God or into other human beings—and without taking adequate safety precautions, I might add. He does not stop to think about what might happen to him if he keeps whirling between the two like that, with one hand pointing up to heaven and the other down to earth.

If he had, he might have been more careful about who he helped. He might not have ventured so far outside the tribe, engaging all kinds of people who could have made him sick, dirty, or suspicious simply by association—people who showed up out of nowhere asking for his help, though many of them did not know the first thing about what he believed or whom *he* asked for help when he left his disciples by the fire at night and went off into the hills to pray.

A disproportionate number of the famous Bible stories about Jesus involve religious strangers—Romans, Samaritans, Canaanites, Syrophoenicians—people who worshipped other gods or worshipped the same one he did in an unorthodox way. These were often the same people who blew Jesus's mind, opening themselves up to what God could do in ways that escaped the people he knew best. When a centurion came seeking help for his servant, Jesus said he had never seen such faith. When a foreign woman came seeking help for her daughter, he praised her faith too. When a Samaritan returned to thank him for a healing, Jesus told him that his faith had made him well. Most Christians who hear such stories assume it is their faith *in him* that he praises, but that is not what the stories say. "*Your* faith," Jesus says to them over and over again. "*Your* faith has made you well." If anything, the strangers seem to change Jesus's ideas about where faith may be found, far outside the boundaries that he has been raised to respect.

Have you ever wondered how he knew people were strangers from a distance? If we can take omniscience off the table for a minute, it was probably the same way you do: by their hair, their skin, their clothing. Before you even get to the gas station clerk who is wearing a turban, you know he is going to speak with an accent. When you are stuck in the pre–happy hour traffic jam at your favorite mall, trying to get out of there before the grid-lock on the expressway starts, the fact that the three young men who saunter in front of your car are wearing baggy shorts and backward baseball caps makes you crazy. They only hold you up for a couple of seconds. You still make the light. If it had been a mother with three children, you would not have thought twice about it, but it was not. It was three young men who seemed to be acting out the same antipathy toward you that you feel toward them.

If these are obvious stereotypes, then that is because clichés zoom to the fore when we are deciding who is in our group and who is not. Remember what Jonathan Sacks said about groupish-ness? According to Michael North, an assistant professor at NYU's Stern School of Business, stereotypes in general—both negative and positive—serve us because they help us take cogni-tive shortcuts. By giving us a way to "automatically categorize people into social groups," they let us "free up mental energy to" live our lives.[2] Left unquestioned, however, they harden into bias that can quickly become a substitute for reality.

Anytime you hear yourself thinking or saying something about "those people," you know that your stranger Geiger coun-ter has just gone off. Without saying a word, simply by being there, the stranger reminds you that you may not know the world as well as you think you do—a world that is full of different peo-ple with different claims on its resources, different notions of right and wrong, and different understandings of God. Without even thinking about it (stereotypes free up mental energy, re-member?), you may conclude that people like you stand to lose something if people who are *not* like you become too powerful, too fearless, or too numerous. Most of the time it only takes one to trigger the problem of the stranger.

This takes me back to Torah, which has far more commands to love the stranger than it does to love the neighbor. The reasons behind those commands range from imitating God to doing what God says, but the reason that comes up most often is remembering what it feels like to be a stranger yourself. "You shall not oppress a stranger, for you know the feelings of the stranger, having yourselves been strangers in the land of Egypt," God says in the book of Exodus. If you get into a situation where you do not have the luxury of thinking about what it means to be authentically human, in other words, all you have to do is remember a time when you were a stranger yourself—when you were on the receiving end of both the derision and the surprising kindness of people who did not look, think, or talk like you. Once it has happened to you, you do not easily forget.

A few summers ago I agreed to meet a friend in the French countryside for a couple of days. I made my first flight, missed the second one, had the next one canceled due to weather, and finally landed at my destination close to midnight. The car rental agency was open for another fifteen minutes, which gave the clerk time to ask me if I could drive a stick shift, hand me the key to a compact car, and wish me, "*Bon voyage.*" Then she locked up the office and left, while I sat in the dark parking lot trying to figure out how to get the voice on the GPS to speak English instead of Czech. When I could not do so, I used my cell phone instead, though I had not signed up for international coverage and would pay dearly for it later.

It seemed like a miracle when my American phone led me directly to the French road that I needed to be on. Then I came to the toll plaza. Since it was after midnight, the only lanes that were open were the automated ones requiring euros I did not have. There was no credit card option. My only two choices were:

(1) back up on the expressway, pull over to the side of the road, and wait until morning; or (2) crash through the barrier and see what happened next. While all of the blood in my body pooled in my feet and a high whine picked up volume in my head, I saw a shadow move in the far left booth.

I backed up the car and drove straight over there to see if my eyes were playing tricks on me—but no! It was a real person, sliding back the glass panel of his dark little booth to look down at me with utter disdain. He said something that almost certainly meant, "What is your problem, lady?" but since I stopped speaking French in high school, I could not answer him. I held out a handful of US quarters instead, piled on top of the hundred-euro note I got from the airport ATM, making the most universal sounds of distress I could manage. It was all my fault, and we both knew it, but he still took pity on me, sliding the hundred-euro note out from under the quarters and coming back moments later with all the change I would need for this toll booth and the others that lay ahead.

"Thank you!" I said. "God bless you!" I said, forgetting that France is a secular country.

"*De rien,*" he said, nodding his head toward the open lane in front of me.

"You go now," he said, while I was still trying to find first gear, making a motion with his hand that meant "shoo" in any language, and I did—though I will never forget the kindness of this particular stranger.

There was nothing remotely life-threatening about my situation. There was so much privilege embedded in it that I should be ashamed to tell you about it at all. The only reason I do is because even something that slight, that frivolous, can come back to mind in some other place, at some other time, when you see another stranger who appears to be lost and in need of help. When that happens, the power of your memory can trump the power of your stereotype, which may include your fear for your own safety. You can decide to pull open your sliding glass door and do what you can, however small a gesture it may be, though there are never any guarantees. Your offer of help may be misguided or rebuffed. You may even get hurt, just as you feared, but there is such liberation in that moment of choosing that the result matters less than the impulse to reach out. When the stranger turns to you with a look of disbelieving gratitude on his face, it matters very much.

"The supreme religious challenge," says Jonathan Sacks, "is to see God's image in one who is not in our image."[3] If he is right, then the stranger—the one who does not look, think, or act like the rest of us—may offer us our best chance at seeing past our own reflections in the mirror to the God we did not make up.

I think it is no mistake that the New Testament never offers a physical description of Jesus. Although most Christians imagine him as the perfect specimen of their own physiognomy, there is nothing in scripture to support that. He might have been short, balding, or bow-legged, more Danny DeVito than Denzel Washington. He almost certainly had bad teeth. Of course, there is nothing in scripture to support that either. All scripture says is that when he appeared to his disciples after his resurrection, few of them recognized him at first. One thought he was the gardener. Others thought he was a fisherman. A couple thought he was a stranger on the road. Even when most of his disciples recognized him, a few still doubted.

That seems just right to me. How wonderful of him to come back undercover, so that even the people who knew him best had to look, then look again, before they got the crawly feeling that they had seen him somewhere before. It was the perfect setup for people who wanted to know what made him different from anyone else they had met: his ability to reflect their humanity back to them, both familiar and strange, so that they never got tired of searching each other's faces for some sign of him. The Son of Man is coming at an unexpected hour, he had told them earlier, so be ready. Little did they know how many hours there were in his day, or that he never rang the bell.

12

The Final Exam

So what do we do? This is our final question.
Whether religion is, for us, a good word or bad;
whether (if on balance it is a good word) we side with
a single religious tradition or to some degree open
our arms to all: How do we comport ourselves in a
pluralistic world that is riven by ideologies, some
sacred, some profane? We listen.

HUSTON SMITH

Fifteen weeks are gone just like that. As often as I have led
this guided tour through the world's great religions, I am
never prepared for it to end. There has been so little time to
explore any of them in depth. There have been so few opportunities to leave the main path. Some days we have covered
thirteen hundred years of history in a single class period. Every time someone has pointed down a compelling side road, I
have looked mournfully down it and said, "I wish we could, but
we don't have time." The Potala Palace in Tibet, the Qumran
Caves by the Dead Sea, the Mormon Temple in Salt Lake City,
the Mother Mosque of America in Cedar Rapids, Iowa—all dis-
appear in the rearview mirror as we speed toward the finish

line. The course is designed to offer students who will only take one course in religion the widest possible exposure, even if that means churning up no more than one inch of topsoil as we go.

Now it is early December, and we are back at the metaphorical parking lot where we began, wondering where the time has gone. I hand back the quizzes students took on the first day of class, so they can see how far they have come.

"I was so wrong," one of them says, looking at the paper in her hand.

"I can't believe that's all I knew," says another. As much as I want to think that the rest are stunned into silence by how much they have learned, the truth is that they are simply ready to go. They have preregistered for the spring semester. They have made plans for the long winter break. They are eyeing their getaway cars, eager to hit the road. The only thing standing in their way is the final exam, which I dread almost as much as they do.

In the beginning, I did unto others what had been done unto me in college: I gave two-hour final exams with multiple-choice, fill-in-the-blank, and matching questions for objective content followed by short-answer questions for subjective responses. Sometimes, when I stayed up too late the night before, I resented having to come up with questions that had right or wrong answers. How could I produce a grading rubric that measured courage or empathy? Where did "increased ability to tolerate existential ambiguity" or "significant gain in spiritual maturity" belong on my bulleted list of course outcomes? It was just as well they were not there, since it was not possible to imagine giving them a letter grade. So I came up with questions that had right or wrong answers instead, though I knew they would cause nothing but misery. Enlightenment was not on the syllabus.

When too many students score lower on their finals than

they have on any of their quizzes, I accept what the results are telling me: it was the experience of the class and not the content of it that was transformative for them. "This was the best class I have taken in college," one student writes at the bottom of his exam, on which he has earned a D. That is why I dread giving final exams—because the grades so seldom reflect the process I have seen taking place.

For fifteen weeks this student and others like him have lived with the kinds of questions that no textbook or teacher can answer. They have considered the often contradictory answers of five great religions, discovering more diversity within the religions than they ever imagined. Their vocabulary list has well over a hundred words on it, in five different languages. Their time line covers four thousand years. By the time they get to the final exam, they have learned so many new things about so many old religions that the lines between them blur.

Do the Four Noble Truths go with Buddhism or Islam?

Does Talmud belong to Hinduism or Judaism?

These are such elementary questions that basic religious literacy depends on remembering the right answers to them, but students do not hang on to the right answers as well as either of us would like. When they leave my class, it is the relationships they remember.

"How is Swami Yogeshananda at the Vedanta Center?" one of them asks me a full year after she has taken the class. "I still think he needs a cat." Another alumnus of the class wants to know if he can go on this semester's field trip to the mosque, since he has thought of another question he wants to ask our guide. A couple engaged to be married return to Drepung Loseling Monastery on their own time to learn more about Medicine Buddha practice. When I show up with a gaggle of students for a field trip one Tuesday night they are already there, sitting in the second row of the dharma hall on square pillows with their legs crossed impressively. Later they will write to let me know they have become Episcopalians and are very active in their church.

Because of them and other students like them, I have added a question about holy envy to the final exam. It comes in the subjective section, where no one gets a D.

A respected religious scholar named Krister Stendahl once formulated three rules for religious understanding that include "Make room for holy envy." What has inspired "holy envy" in you this semester?

"I have been ignited by holy envy in a lot of ways," one student writes in response. "I love the notion that karma is not measured or judged by a higher power; you are responsible for your own actions. Whether I decide to believe in a religion or not, I will keep this moral code of self-accountability with me."

Another says she has been inspired by the writings of the Dalai Lama. "I envy his deep belief in compassion and genuine love for all humanity," she writes. "I wish Christians would focus on being more compassionate instead of feeling like they have to correct everyone else."

One student recounts the same experience that inspired holy envy in me:

When it comes to holy envy, one thing really sticks out in my mind. When we went to the mosque on our field trip, the imam spoke to us ahead of time, and what he told us is my holy envy. He told us how he doesn't wish to convert us to Islam. He just wants us to be the best people we can be, regardless of religion. This was the most beautiful thing I have ever heard, and it's my holy envy because I wish Christianity was this way.

While the students are still finishing their exams, I look down at their names in my grade book. Some have already sold their textbooks back to the bookstore, replacing them with volumes on cellular biology, intermediate Spanish, criminal justice, or computer science. As soon as I post their grades, world religions will lose most of its color, fading in their memories along with world history and world literature. A few will keep the Buddhist mandalas they created for class or the bumper stickers I handed out before the unit on Islam ("Don't Believe Everything You Think"). A few might even sign up for another religion class, but this one has come to an end. In a matter of weeks I will be greeting a new room full of students, welcoming them to Religion 101.

It is a repeating loop that has inspired my best efforts for years, which means that my education has loops in it too. Every semester I tinker with the syllabus, searching for ways to simplify the content and deepen the engagement, to bring the world into the classroom and the class into the world. I have done it so often that I do not need the sheet music anymore. I can play it by heart. But that is the treble line of the course, which starts over again every fifteen weeks. The bass line is something else altogether—a low, insistent strain that does not stop when the class ends but is there when I wake up in the morning and is still there when I go to sleep at night. It is the sound of my own unknowing going forward like an underground current headed toward an ocean for which I have no name.

Teaching the course has enriched my soul in so many ways.

It has also shaken many of my foundations. Now when I explain to students why Jews do not believe Jesus was the messiah, the reasons make sense to me. When I tell the story of the night Muhammad received the first verses of the Qur'an in a cave outside of Mecca, I believe that the angel Gabriel stood in attendance. When I spell out the ways in which the Hindu concept of Brahman differs from the Christian concept of God, the Hindu concept strikes me as far more advanced. When I teach the Buddha's Four Noble Truths, they sound perfectly true.

Spending extended amounts of time inside other religious worldviews has loosened the screws on my own, which is beginning to seem like a good thing. Disowning God has been a great help to me. Owning my distinct view of God has helped me understand it much better. Although I can see the places where religious truth claims collide, this does not bother me as much as it could. I am far more interested in how people live than what they believe. When other Christians threaten or disappoint me, I work as hard to see God in them as in people of other (or no) faiths. It helps to remember that these are often the same Christians whom I threaten and disappoint in equal measure. The only clear line I draw these days is this: when my religion tries to come between me and my neighbor, I will choose my neighbor. That self-canceling feature of my religion is one of the things I like best about it. Jesus never commanded me to love my religion.

There are losses as well, of course. For as long as I can remember, I have been on the lookout for a solid place to stand with God. Sometimes that search has taken me to a literal place, such as a church, where people seem confident in the way they speak of and bow down to God. Other times the search has cost me a fortune in books. When I was sure the answer to my predicament was in the Bible, I invested thousands of dollars in commentaries and theories of interpretation. When I was sure the answer was in the medieval mystics, I filled my shelves with their works and those of the scholars who knew them best. For a while I thought the answer might be in process theology, or the poetry of R. S. Thomas, or the regular practice of morning and evening prayer.

All of this has been very helpful, but none of it has delivered me to a solid place with God. If anything, it has increased the squishiness underfoot, by offering me so many different ways of seeing the divine that I feel like a fly with compound eyes. When I began teaching world religions, I gained so many new lenses that it was a wonder I could walk in a straight line. Is God one or three or thirty-three thousand? Do people suffer more from sin or from ignorance? Is God a divine being who moves human beings around or a field of cosmic consciousness in which all things align? What do I mean when I say "God"? When this becomes too much for me, I remember what I tell the students. "If it is God you want, look for the light and not the diamond. There are so many facets, and yet the light is not in any of them. Their beauty lies in their ability to reflect what is beyond them."

When I first began teaching Religion 101, students would sometimes tell me they were scared to study other religions for fear of losing their faith. It was an odd concern, on the face of it. Would studying Spanish make them lose their English? Would traveling to Turkey cost them their US passport? I had a stock response to their concern: engaging the faith of others is the best way to grow your own.

Now, years down the road, I have greater respect for their unease. To discover that your faith is one among many—that there are hundreds of others that have sustained millions of people for thousands of years, and that some of them make a great deal of sense—that can rock your boat, especially if you thought yours was the only one on the sea. If your faith depends on being God's only child, then the discovery that there are others can lead you to decide that someone must be wrong—or that everyone belongs, which means that no religion, including yours, is the entire ocean.

The next time I teach the course I will try to be more honest. "Engaging the faith of others will almost certainly cause you to lose faith in the old box you kept God in," I will say. "The truths you glimpse in other religions are going to crowd up against some of your own. Holy envy may lead you to borrow some things, and you will need a place to put them. You may find spiritual guides outside your box whom you want to make room for, or some neighbors from other faiths who have stopped by for a visit. However it happens, your old box will turn out to be too small for who you have become. You will need a bigger one with more windows in it—something more like a home than a box, perhaps—where you can open the door to all kinds of people without fearing their faith will cancel yours out if you let them in. If things go well, they may invite you to visit them in their homes as well, so that your children can make friends."

After I say good-bye to this semester's students, I go home with their papers under my arm, thinking about the final exam Jesus proposed near the end of his life. He too seemed more interested in how people lived than what they believed. When his death was before him and he knew it, Matthew says, he told his disciples what to expect when the Son of Man comes in his glory and all the angels with him.

It will be as if he were sitting on his throne looking out at all the people of all the nations in the world, Matthew says—still a shepherd, though now also a king—faced with the final duty of separating the sheep in the flock from the goats. They will have grazed together for ages by then—eaten the same grass, drunk from the same streams, slept under the same stars—but at last it will be time for the metaphorical goats to go one way and the sheep to go another. If you can remember the "metaphorical" part, the story is easier to hear.

Surprisingly, none of the people standing before the throne will know which one they are, perhaps because this is the first time they have heard the Son of Man lay out the criteria for their separation. Some may have thought that what they believed about him would make all the difference. Others may have hoped that being with him from the start would mean that they had tenured positions in the flock.

Whatever they think, he will surprise them. Sheep and goats, he will surprise them, because in the end the criteria for telling them apart will have nothing to do with their beliefs or their allegiances and everything to do with how they have treated the least important people in their lives—the ones who were shoved so far to the side that no one even saw them anymore; the ones who had been treated as if they were guilty of something for so long that acting guilty had seeped into them like smog; the ones who were too sick to return the favor, too old to say thank you, too strange to feel safe around, too hard to help.

It was me you ignored, the king will tell the unsuspecting goats. *It was me you passed by*. This will come as a huge shock to those who thought they knew for sure what he looked like (blond hair, blue robe, right?), who kept tabs on his whereabouts and stayed as close to him as they could, once they suspected who he was. "Lord, when was it that we saw you?" That is what they will not be able to figure out. Had he been wearing a red wig, a fake nose, a hoodie? How had they, of all people, failed to recognize their Lord and come quickly to his aid?

His answer to their questions will come too late for them. It was a case of mistaken identity, yes, but not the way they had conceived it. Their mistake was to think that he lived in one body, not all bodies; that he lived behind one face, not all faces; that he saw them through one set of eyes, not all sets of eyes. But what is terrible news for some will be wonderful news for others:

> Then the king will say to those at his right hand, "Come, you that are blessed by my Father, inherit the kingdom prepared for you from the foundation of the world; for I was hungry and you gave me food, I was thirsty and you gave me something to drink, I was a stranger and you welcomed me, I was naked and you gave me clothing, I was sick and you took care of me, I was in prison and you visited me." Then the righteous will answer him, "Lord, when was it that we saw you . . . ?" (Matt. 25:34–37)

If you know this passage as well as I do, you may have to slow down and count all of the king's disguises as they go by: hungry person, thirsty person, strange person, naked person, sick person, imprisoned person. How many did you get right? I do not know why so many people skip over the strange person, but they do. Yet there it is. One of the ways the Son of Man smuggles himself into our midst is by showing up as a stranger in need of welcome. *Welcome* is the king's solution to the problem of the stranger. Always has been, always will be.

That is where I have ended up anyway. Just like my students, it is not the facts I remember but the relationships: the Hindu swami who calls me some Sunday afternoons just to ask how

I am getting along; the Muslim imam who came to church to hear me talk and helped me with my Arabic pronunciation when I faltered; the Buddhist monk who sends me Christmas cards every year; the Reform rabbi who wishes me a blessed Advent. This is about them, not me, but the joke is definitely on me.

I asked God for religious certainty, and God gave me relationships instead. I asked for solid ground, and God gave me human beings instead—strange, funny, compelling, complicated human beings—who keep puncturing my stereotypes, challenging my ideas, and upsetting my ideas about God, so that they are always under construction. I may yet find the answer to all my questions in a church, a book, a theology, or a practice of prayer, but I hope not. I hope God is going to keep coming to me in authentically human beings who shake my foundations, freeing me to go deeper into the mystery of *why we are all here*.

Meanwhile, it helps to remember that neither the sheep nor the goats in Matthew's parable knew which one they were. They were all on the sacred way of unknowing. The sheep were as surprised to learn they had done something *right* as the goats were to learn they had done something *wrong*. None of them had recognized the king in their midst. His clever disguises had fooled them all. The only thing that set them apart, in the end, was that half of them had made a habit of treating everyone they met with kindness and respect—even the ungrateful ones, even the ones that scared them—and that made all the difference.

The God I believe in does not send half the flock to slaughter for bad behavior (though the Jesus I believe in is not above telling a story like that to shock his listeners awake), which is why I like to ride the metaphor all the way. If the sheep and the goats in the story are really people, then why can't the people in the story be part sheep and part goat? Does anyone behave the same way all the time? Is anyone purely good or bad?

The Russian novelist and Nobel Prize winner Aleksandr Solzhenitsyn did not think so. In *The Gulag Archipelago* he wrote:

> If only it were all so simple! If only there were evil people somewhere insidiously committing evil deeds, and it were necessary only to separate them from the rest of us and destroy them. But the line dividing good and evil cuts through the heart of every human being. And who is willing to destroy a piece of his own heart?[1]

The key phrase here is "every human being." That is my baseline for becoming Christian, anyway—to extend the same care to every human being that I wish for myself, to treat every human being as if he or she were Jesus in disguise. I will surely flunk this exam, but I am also willing to be surprised. Who knows? Maybe a day will come when the sheep and the goats lie down together, purring like cats at the feet of the divine stranger who has put all their fears to rest.

Epilogue:
Church of the Common Ground

It is a great mistake to suppose that God is only, or even chiefly, concerned with religion.

ARCHBISHOP WILLIAM TEMPLE

In the middle of writing this book I decided to retire from teaching religion. During the months that followed, my feelings mimicked those of empty nesters suddenly faced with a quiet house and no young energy to govern. Students of all ages had brought me so much delight through the years—such real questions, such uncensored reactions, such spontaneous humor and natural affection—that there was no substitute for them in my life. I kept waiting to tire of teaching them, but it never happened. To the very last, they called forth my best efforts and repaid them by being thoroughly themselves. They forgave me my bad days as I forgave them theirs. On our good days, there was no better place to be than the classroom, where we changed each other in ways that still matter.

At the same time, I was ready to let someone else teach the world's great religions. The longer I did it, the more dishonest I felt. Fifteen weeks was not enough time to do justice to even one of them. The only way to get through five that fast was to desiccate them, reducing each to its skeletal outline with enough

names and dates to anchor a ten-point quiz. In my effort to present the best of each tradition, I often sent students away with
positive stereotypes that served them no better than negative
ones. Every time we went on a field trip to a place of worship or
devotion, I wondered how wise it was to split religion off from
the rest of life. Why didn't we go to a girls' basketball game at a
Muslim high school instead, or invite an entire Hindu family to
class? Even the textbook treated religions like sealed compart-
ments that could be kept separate from one another, each with
its own glossary at the end.

Something I learned in college came back to me with force.
There is no such thing as *religion*. There are only religious *people*,
who embody the scripts of their faiths as differently as dancers
embody the steps of their dances. Until someone grabs a partner
and heads to the dance floor, the tango is no more than a list of
steps on the wall. The same is true of faith. We have inherited a
sacred pattern, a series of artful steps meant to lead us closer to
God and each other, but until someone finds a partner and gives
it a try, it is an idea and not a dance.

What this means is that is it not possible for a generic group
of Christians to meet with a generic group of Buddhists to discuss a generic issue on which they differ.[1] If you have met one
Buddhist, you have met exactly one—and the same is true of the
followers of other faiths as well. Although we may all be tuned
to the singular teachings of our distinct religions, our religious
experience is not singular but plural. This is as true within our
religions as it is between them.

That was the key insight for me, back when I was failing
Christianity. Once I fully accepted that there are mutually ex-
clusive views of what it means to be Christian—that Catholic,
Orthodox, and Protestant Christians of good faith can disagree

about a great many things without being forced off the dance floor, and that God alone is competent to judge their performances—it was only a short step from there to accepting that there are mutually exclusive views of the divine mystery as well, among which I am not competent to judge. All I can do is dance my heart out, finding as much to admire in the other dancers as I do in those who dance with me.

Though I am retired from teaching religion, I am not done searching the scriptures, history, and tradition of my faith for good reasons to engage other people in theirs. Some days I do it because I want to be a peacemaker. Other days I do it because I am starved for the God I did not make up. In either case, I often find myself at what Richard Rohr calls "the edge of the inside" of my tradition, where I can keep an eye on the door. After half a lifetime near the center and no wish to be outside, being eccentric suits me in the truest sense of the word. It suits me to be off center, sometimes pressed against the edges of my tradition like a kid on the Gravitron at the county fair.

Rohr explains that being on the edge of the inside is not a rebellious position any more than it is an antisocial one. "When you live on the edge of anything with respect and honor," he says, "you are in a very auspicious and advantageous position. You are free of its central seductions, but also free to hear its core message in very new and creative ways."[2] Since I know how quickly my ego warms to advantageous positions, I appreciate David Brooks's warning about the downsides of living at the edge in his column for the *New York Times*. "You never lose yourself in a full commitment," he says. "You may be respected and befriended, but you are not loved as completely as the people at the core, the band of brothers. You enjoy neither the purity of the outsider nor that of the true believer."[3]

He is right about that. Yet the best reason to stay put, he says, is because reality looks different from the inside of the edge. People who are all the way in or all the way out tend to think in terms of "us" versus "them," but from the perspective of the edge it is possible to see how the two may actually be in relationship with each other and with some larger process, even when it does not look that way to either of them.[4] "A doorkeeper must love both the inside and the outside of his or her group," Rohr adds, "and know how to move between those two loves."

John Philip Newell offers a different way of thinking about how to navigate the distance between the center and the edge of faith. Sometimes you just have to pack your bag and go. Early in the Christian story, he says, Celtic monks living in the British Isles engaged in the practice of peregrination, which involved the deliberate decision to leave home for parts unknown. The word "peregrine" comes from an old Latin word for "foreigner" or "pilgrim," as in the peregrine falcon, which can fly from the Arctic Circle to South America and back again in a single year, or St. Brendan the Navigator, the sixth-century Irish monk who spent seven years on the sea in a hide-covered boat searching for the legendary island of Paradise. Early Christians sometimes described peregrination as "seeking the place of one's resurrection," Newell says, since it meant dying to their old boundaries in order to find new life out beyond the buoys.[5]

I plan to keep that practice up, even if it does not involve an actual boat. I want to keep leaving my comfort zone on a regular basis in order to visit the neighbors, without expecting them to exemplify their faith any better than I exemplify mine. I also want to keep pressing the boundaries of my own faith, which can turn into walls if I let them. Recently my neighbor installed an electric fence to keep his old German shepherd and his new golden Lab from running away. Every time I see them inside their yard with their shock collars on, barking a safe three feet away from the white flags that mark the hotwire buried underneath, I feel a sting in my neck.

My holy envy has taken an interesting turn in recent months, as the practice of peregrination has led me to explore different churches in my own faith. My best friend, Martha, has joined me in these voyages, which have taken us from the huge Passion City megachurch, which meets in an old Home Depot, to Our Lady of Lourdes, the mother church of African-American Catholics in Atlanta. One Sunday we visited a tiny storefront church in a strip mall with people from many nations inside, tended by an Episcopal priest from South Asia. Another Sunday we sat quietly with the Quakers. Still on our list are St. Elias Antiochian Orthodox Church, Ebenezer Baptist Church, and the Buckhead Church, where members watch a hologram of their pastor preaching from one of the six other churches in his network.

I have found something to envy every place I have been— the parking-lot hospitality at Passion City, the graceful dancers who waved banners of red silk over our heads at Our Lady of Lourdes, the refugee ministry at the storefront church, the blissful stillness of the Quakers. But none has compared to my first experience of the Church of the Common Ground, which meets at a public park in the heart of downtown Atlanta. "We're like any other church," their website reads. "We just don't have a building." I envy that.

The crowd was bigger than usual on the day I visited, since the bishop was coming to help welcome the new vicar, an Episcopal priest named Monica. I recognized a few people from my old congregation down the street, a classically beautiful and well-endowed parish named All Saints. There were also a lot of people who looked as if they had spent the night on the street. When I asked a Native American man with a gray ponytail how long he had been a member of Common Ground, he said, "Years." Trying to make conversation, I told him I had started at All Saints down the street. "Well," he said, in an obvious effort to be kind, "we all have to start somewhere."

A small wooden table covered with a white cloth had been set up for Communion in the middle of the park. Behind us, a wall of water ran down the side of a public fountain. Blackbirds flew between the trees overhead. When the bishop had arrived and most of the regular members were accounted for, the man with the gray ponytail held up a brass gong and banged it lightly, summoning us all to gather around the table. I found my place at the edge of the inside and surveyed the array of faces around the circle: the father holding his premature baby, the teenager with the uneven skull, the couple in their seventies whom I knew from All Saints, and the man with the rusty beard who had lost all his front teeth, along with Monica's husband, Simon, holding the hand of their youngest child. There must have been close to a hundred people in all, representing a divine swath of the human condition.

We had just gotten started when a loud voice from the back rose above all of the others. "Liars!" a woman's voice shrieked. "This is all lies, lies, lies!" As she pushed her way through the crowd toward the middle, it became apparent—at least to me—that she was in her right mind. She was African American, about five foot four. She wore nice sweatpants, a navy hoodie over a ball cap, and reflective aviator sunglasses. With her trendy pink backpack, she could have been a student at Georgia State University across the street. She did not look or sound crazy. She just looked and sounded really mad.

"Wake up, people!' she screamed. "This god you're praying to, what does he look like? *What does he look like?*" She spat each word out as though it had a period at the end. "They are killing us all day long, people. You *know* they are, and here you are praying to their God! What do you think that's going to change? It's all lies, lies, lies!" As she ran this tirade a couple more times at high volume, people in the congregation started talking back to her.

"You need to step back now," a man said. "You're in my space."

"Take your rant somewhere else," someone else said. "This is a peaceful place."

"There's always one," another person said.

The bishop had tried to begin his sermon once, but the woman had drowned him out. Since he is the first African-American bishop of the Episcopal Diocese of Atlanta, her smack talk about God fell short of its mark. To his credit, the bishop just folded his hands over his vestments and stood in front of the Communion table waiting for her to wind down. A minute later, a man in a red and blue jacket and a bicycle helmet rode up to the back of the crowd on a Segway. When he started walking toward the woman, she quieted down. When he reached her, she turned and followed him out of the crowd. His jacket had "Ambassador" written in big block letters on the back. I had not been this awake in church in years.

"One of the great things about Church of the Common Ground is that there are no walls," the bishop said when he resumed his sermon. "This is where the church meets the world." Everyone around me nodded and hummed their approval when he said that. Then they listened to him so quietly that I could hear the sound of the water running down the wall of the fountain behind me. The angry woman was still standing at the back of the crowd talking to the ambassador.

The bishop did not put her on the spot by looking at her, but he included her when he said, "There is nothing to prevent us from hearing the real concerns other people have about us, some of the legitimate questions they have about who we are and what we do. We need to listen to them too, so it is good that we are here, with no walls to keep us in or shut them out. What better way to remember that we really are one?"

There it was again—the "one" word, the expressed faith in Christian unity—only this time it sounded different to me.

"As different as we are," the bishop said, "whatever concerns we bring, we are all one."

Coming from him, in that place, with those people, I hoped it was true. I wanted it to be true. He said more after that, but pretty soon it was as if his words were coming out of the mouths of the people all around me. I could not separate what he was saying from the sea of human beings who proved the truth of it—not just the ones in the Christian circle, but also the ones walking by on Peachtree Street still dozy from brunch, the ones still rolled up in sleeping bags over by the fountain, and the ones I could see looking down on us from some office windows higher up. Were they janitors or executives? There was no way to tell. All I could tell, looking up, was that there was no ceiling on this church either. The sky just went on and on.

After we had all joined hands and listened to each other's prayers, the new vicar invited us to come closer to the Communion table. I left my spot at the back and got as close to the table as I could. This was partly because I wanted to be one of the first to sip from the common cup—I'm just saying—but it was also because this was the only church in a long time that had drawn me to the center. I looked around to make sure I was not blocking anyone else's view. The man with the rusty beard and no front teeth was on my left. A woman with platinum hair and a sparkly cap with "The Ministry Team" written across it was on my right. When the vicar finally held out the bread to me, it was as sweet as honey in my mouth. So was the grape juice. Then I must have sailed to the island of paradise, because I do not remember much after that. There was nothing left to envy. I was exactly where I wanted to be.

At the end, after the vicar gave the final blessing, I saw the angry woman standing under a tree at the back of the crowd with a pleasant-looking man from the community. She had kept her back turned to us the whole time. She never showed us her face again, but she never left either. Did that put her at the outer edge of the inside or the inner edge of the outside? Wherever she was, she was still there, nodding at something the man was saying, so that her pink backpack bobbed up and down.

Just before I left to go back to my car, a fresh wind blew up out of nowhere and tossed the leaves of the trees around, sending the blackbirds scattering with loud cries. Then they settled down on new branches, watching as the church below them drifted back into the world again, all of us blinking in the sunlight of a brand-new day.

Acknowledgments

Where shall I begin? Obviously, with the hundreds of Piedmont students who taught me how to teach world religions by being their curious, straightforward, and tender selves. Among those who allowed me to tell their stories are Bryan Schroeder, Tim Hudson, Madison Marcus, and Joel Rodriguez. Other students will be happy that I did not mention them by name, though I hope they will recognize themselves here, since that is how they will know what important roles they played in my education.

Patrick Reid earns double acknowledgment for being the first reader of this manuscript as well as a front-row student in Religion 101. His ability to navigate both of those roles speaks volumes about his character. Patrick is now a student at Yale Divinity School, where he continues to impress his teachers with his racehorse mind, his generous heart, and his ready humor.

Catherine Owers also read this manuscript from beginning to end, giving me helpful guidance that led to significant revisions. Tom Grady, Mickey Maudlin, and Anna Paustenbach read enough different versions to make them all crazy. I count it a great mercy that they are all still speaking to me.

There is no bottom to my gratitude to the people who welcomed Piedmont students into their most sacred places through the years, often at the expense of taking time off from their real jobs: Swami Yogeshananda and Brother Shankara at the Vedanta Center of Atlanta; the monks and members of Drepung Loseling Monastery; the volunteer teachers of the Tuesday night open house at Shambhala Meditation Center; Rabbi Peter Berg, Rabbi Loren Filson Lapidus, Cantor Deborah Hartman, and Ronnie van Gelder at the Temple; Imam Plemon El-Amin and Imam Sulaimaan Hamed at the Atlanta Masjid of Al-Islam; Bilal Mahmud and Dr. Khalid Siddiq at Al-Farooq Masjid, along with other generous hosts at the Greek Orthodox Cathedral of the Annunciation, the Episcopal Cathedral of St. Philip, and the Cistercian Monastery of the Holy Spirit.

If you have read this far, then you already know the names of the people I read regularly and admire most for leading the way in a new religious America. Their published work is collected in the recommended reading section of this book. Yet there are only a few whom I have met in person, who were willing to speak with me at any length about the subject of this book: Diana Eck, Eboo Patel, Laurie Patton, John Philip Newell, Lucinda Mosher, and Rami Shapiro. Jan Swanson, longtime program director of the World Pilgrims program, has also inspired me for decades. I am very grateful to all of these trailblazers for the work they are doing in this world, and for giving themselves so generously to conversations with people like me.

I also owe a word of thanks to my hosts at a variety of public venues, who encouraged me to present earlier versions of chapters in this book to live audiences. They include Buzzy Pickren,

Billie Sargent, and Peter McCall of January Adventure; Randy and Pat Robertson of Gladdening Light; Ann Holtz and Fran McKendree of Awakening Soul; Bill Saling of Mountaintop Lectures; Barbara Lund of Wisdom Ways; Cathy Zappa of the Episcopal Cathedral of St. Philip; Helen Blier and Shan Overton of Pittsburgh Theological Seminary; Nancy McGrath of Sunriver Christian Fellowship; and John Randolph of the Palm Beach Fellowship of Christians and Jews.

Members of my family and friendship circle who appear in these pages include Martha Sterne, Judy Barber, Ava Mills, and Monica Mainwaring, all of whom have expanded my thinking about faith as well as the spaciousness of my heart.

Laina Adler, Anna Paustenbach, Jenn Jensen, Suzanne Wickham, Lisa Zuniga, Ann Moru, Yvonne Chan, Michelle Crowe, and Ann Edwards at HarperOne have all been vital to the publication of this book. I love working with these women, and am thankful for the ways in which each has exercised her considerable skills on my behalf. A long-stemmed red rose to each of you.

Having saved the best for last, I now come to Tom Grady, who has been my literary rock and trusted friend for more than a decade. Though we are seldom in the same room together, he can change my entire outlook on a book that is going south by giving it a firm nudge in a new direction and propping me up with prodigal encouragement. I cannot thank him often enough. Mickey Maudlin has been my editor for the same length of time, doing all the heavy lifting of getting four books out of my head and into the world. This has often required courageous intervention by him since I am as protective of my prose as a hen of her chick. He has persevered with a saving mix of editorial insight and true camaraderie, for which I am exceedingly grateful. Although Mark Tauber has moved on from HarperOne, he took me under his wing from the first time we met and remains one of my favorite people in the world. So does Claudia Boutote.

I am also thankful to you, dear reader, for buying books, filling them with your notes, discussing them, reviewing them, and recommending them to your friends. As important as religious literacy has become to me, everyday literacy still takes first place. The more we read, the wider our worlds become. The more books we love, the larger our hearts grow. May your tribe—and the fortunes of independent booksellers—increase.

And then there is Ed. What is left to say? There is no one in the world who gets me, upholds me, challenges me, or teaches me as much as he does. I cannot imagine life without him, and I thank God I do not have to.

Notes

CHAPTER 1

1. Donald E. Chapman, "Estevanico," Texas State Historical Association, accessed August 15, 2018, https://tshaonline.org/handbook/online/articles/fes08/.

2. "Early American Mosques," *The Pluralism Project*, Harvard University, accessed February 2, 2018, http://pluralism.org/religions/islam/islam-in-america/early-american-mosques/.

3. "Hinduism in America," *The Pluralism Project*, Harvard University, accessed February 2, 2018, http://pluralism.org/timeline/hinduism-in-america/.

4. "Buddhists in the American West," *The Pluralism Project*, Harvard University, accessed February 2, 2018, http://pluralism.org/religions/buddhism/buddhism-in-america/buddhists-in-the-american-west/.

5. "Charleston, South Carolina," *Encyclopedia of Southern Jewish Communities* (Goldring/Woldenberg Institute of Southern Jewish Life, 2017), accessed February 2, 2018; http://www.isjl.org/south-carolina-charleston-encyclopedia.html.

6. "The Immigration Act of 1924 (The Johnson-Reed Act)," Office of the Historian, accessed March 31, 2018. https://history.state.gov /milestones/1921-1936/immigration-act.

CHAPTER 2

1. "Lord of the Dance," words: Sydney Carter, Copyright © 1963 Stainer & Bell, Ltd. (Admin. Hope Publishing Company, Carol Stream, IL 60188). All rights reserved. Used by permission.
2. Paul Dilley, "Jesus as Lord of the Dance," *Bible History Daily*, August 15, 2016, https://www.biblicalarchaeology.org/daily /biblical-topics/post-biblical-period/jesus-as-lord-of-the-dance/.
3. Ian Bradley, *Daily Telegraph Book of Hymns* (London: Continuum, 2005), 185.
4. Sydney Carter, "Lord of the Dance," © 1963, Stainer & Bell, Ltd. (Admin. Hope Publishing Company, Carol Stream, IL 60188).

CHAPTER 3

1. Martin Palmer, *The Jesus Sutras: Rediscovering the Lost Scrolls of Taoist Christianity* (New York: Wellspring/Ballantine, 2001).
2. Paul F. Knitter, *Without Buddha I Could Not Be a Christian* (Oxford: Oneworld, 2009), 216.
3. Eboo Patel, *Acts of Faith* (Boston: Beacon, 2007), 94.

CHAPTER 4

1. Douglas Martin, "Krister Stendahl, 86, Ecumenical Bishop, Is Dead," *New York Times*, April 16, 2008.
2. Farīd ud-Dīn 'Aṭṭār, and A. J. Arberry, "Rabe'a al-Adawiya," *in Muslim Saints and Mystics: Episodes from the Tadhkirat al-Auliya* (Chicago: University of Chicago Press, 1966), 51.
3. Yehezkel Landau, "An Interview with Krister Stendahl," *Harvard Divinity Bulletin*, Winter 2007.
4. "The Buddha's Farewell," Internet Sacred Text Archive, accessed April 1, 2018, http://www.sacred-texts.com/bud/btg /btg94.htm.

5.   Robert Farrar Capon, *Hunting the Divine Fox: Images and Mystery in Christian Faith* (New York: Seabury, 1974), 1.

6.   Richard Rohr, in a lecture given during the 2017 Gladdening Light Symposium in Winter Park, FL, January 26–29, 2017. For a close approximation in print, see https://cac.org/living-word-god-2018 -01-17.

7.   J. Hick and P. F. Knitter, eds., "The Jordan, the Tiber, and the Ganges: Three Kairological Moments of Christic Self-Consciousness," in *The Myth of Christian Uniqueness: Toward a Pluralistic Theology of Religions* (Maryknoll, NY: Orbis Books, 1987), 89–116.

CHAPTER 5

1.   Jonathan Sacks, *The Dignity of Difference*, rev. ed. (London: Continuum, 2003), 60.

2.   Barbara Barkley, "Understanding Christian Fundamentalism," *The Thoughtful Christian*, September 12, 2007, http://www .thethoughtfulchristian.com/Products/TC0208/understanding -christian-fundamentalism.aspx.

CHAPTER 6

1.   "Crown Him with Many Crowns," lyrics by Matthew Bridges (1800–1894), *The Hymnal 1982* (New York: Church Hymnal Corporation), 494.

2.   Isa. 45:1–6. For more about these characters and others, see Jeffrey Salkin, *Righteous Gentiles in the Hebrew Bible* (Woodstock, VT: Jewish Lights, 2008).

CHAPTER 7

1.   Michael Lipka, "How Many People of Different Faiths Do You Know?" *Pew Research Center*, July 17, 2014, http://www .pewresearch.org/fact-tank/2014/07/17/how-many-people-of -different-faiths-do-you-know/.

2.   Kate Kellaway, "Claudia Rankine: Blackness in the White Imagination Has Nothing to Do with Black People," *The*

Guardian, December 27, 2015, https://www.theguardian.com
/books/2015/dec/27/claudia-rankine-poet-citizen-american-lyric
-feature.

3. Jonathan Sacks, *Not in God's Name: Confronting Religious Violence* (New York: Schocken, 2015), 11.

4. Sacks, *Not in God's Name*, 40–41.

5. Byron L. Sherwin, "Who Do You Say That I Am?" in Beatrice Bruteau, ed., *Jesus Through Jewish Eyes* (Maryknoll, NY: Orbis Books, 2001), 39. For a more in-depth survey of the other views mentioned, see Gregory A. Barker, ed., *Jesus in the World's Faiths* (Maryknoll, NY: Orbis Books, 2005).

6. Linda K. Wertheimer, *Faith Ed: Teaching About Religion in an Age of Intolerance* (Boston: Beacon, 2016), 39–70.

7. "Organization," Al-Farooq Masjid of Atlanta, accessed August 15, 2016, http://alfarooqmasjid.org/about-us/organization/.

8. For details, see Carl W. Ernst, "From the Heart of the Qur'an Belt," *Religious Studies News*, May 2003, accessed February 28, 2018, http://www.unc.edu/~cernst/rsnews.htm.

9. Ryan Broderick, "A Lot of People Are Very Upset That an Indian-American Woman Won the Miss America Pageant," *BuzzFeed News*, September 16, 2013, https://www.buzzfeed .com/ryanhatesthis/a-lot-of-people-are-very-upset-that -an-indian-american-woman?utm_term=.emWlkEoVq# .geNm01B2M.

CHAPTER 8

1. Pearl S. Buck, *My Several Worlds: A Personal Record* (New York: Pocket Books, 1956), 56.

2. M. K. Gandhi, *The Message of Jesus Christ*, ed. Anand T. Hingorani (Bombay: Bharatiya Vidya Bhavan, 1986), 44.

3. "Matthew 5–7: The Sermon on the Mount and India," by R. S. Sugirtharajah, in Daniel Patte, *Global Bible Commentary* (Nashville: Abingdon, 2004), 365.

4. Amy-Jill Levine, *The Misunderstood Jew* (San Francisco: HarperOne, 2006), 92–93.

5. Barbara Bradley Hagerty, "Surviving the Wasteland of Faith," *Christianity Today*, November 23, 2016.

6. Jonathan Sacks, *The Dignity of Difference*, rev. ed. (London: Continuum, 2003), 8.

CHAPTER 9

1. "2010 Presidential Medal of Freedom Recipient—Maya Angelou," video, The White House: President Barack Obama, February 16, 2011, https://obamawhitehouse.archives.gov/photos-and-video /video/2011/02/16/2010-presidential-medal-freedom-recipient -maya-angelou/.

2. These theologians include Jürgen Moltmann, Sallie McFague, Hans Küng, Donald Gelpi, Elizabeth A. Johnson, Michael Lodahl, Peter Hodgson, and many, many others.

CHAPTER 10

1. Midrash ha-Gadol 11:3, as cited in W. Gunther Plaut, ed., *The Torah: A Modern Commentary* (New York: Union of American Hebrew Congregations, 1981), 85.

2. In Plaut, ed. *The Torah*, 85

3. Jonathan Sacks, *The Dignity of Difference*, rev. ed. (London: Continuum, 2003), 2.

CHAPTER 11

1. Paul C. Rosenblatt, "Grief in Small-Scale Societies," in Colin Murray Parkes, Pittu Laungani, and Bill Young, eds., *Death and Bereavement Across Cultures* (London and New York: Routledge, 2015), 38.

2. Anne Tergesen, "To Age Well, Change How You Feel About Aging," *Wall Street Journal*, October 19, 2015.

3. Jonathan Sacks, *The Dignity of Difference*, rev. ed. (London: Continuum, 2003), 60.

CHAPTER 12

1. Aleksandr Solzhenitsyn, *The Gulag Archipelago 1918–1956* (New York: Harper & Row, 1974), 168.

EPILOGUE

1. See Wilfred Cantwell Smith, *The Meaning and End of Religion*, or, more recently, *Patterns of Faith Around the World*, with thanks to Eboo Patel for verbalizing this central truth.
2. Richard Rohr, "On the Edge of the Inside: The Prophetic Position," from *The Eight Core Principles of the Center for Action and Contemplation* (out of print); for the eight core principles, see https://cac.org/about-cac/missionvision/.
3. David Brooks, "At the Edge of the Inside," *New York Times*, June 24, 2016, https://www.nytimes.com/2016/06/24/opinion/at-the -edge-of-inside.html.
4. Brooks, "At the Edge of the Inside."
5. John Philip Newell, *The Rebirthing of God: Christianity's Struggle for New Beginnings* (Woodstock, VT: Skylight Paths, 2014), 45.

Recommended Reading

Albright, Madeleine. *The Mighty and the Almighty: Reflections on God, America, and World Affairs.* HarperPerennial, 2007.

Barker, Gregory A. *Jesus in the World's Faiths: Leading Thinkers from Five Religions Reflect on His Meaning.* Orbis Books, 2008.

Barker, Gregory A. and Stephen E. Gregg. *Jesus Beyond Christianity: The Classic Texts.* Oxford, 2010.

The Dalai Lama. *Toward a True Kinship of Faiths: How the World's Religions Can Come Together.* Doubleday Religion, 2010.

Epstein, Greg M. *Good Without God: What a Billion Nonreligious People Do Believe.* William Morrow, 2010.

Griffiths, Bede. *The Cosmic Revelation: The Hindu Way to God.* Collins, 1983.

Gross, Rita M. *Buddhists Talk about Jesus, Christians Talk about the Buddha.* Continuum, 2003.

Hick, John, and Paul F. Knitter. *The Myth of Christian Uniqueness: Toward a Pluralistic Theology of Religions.* Orbis Books, 1987.

Knitter, Paul F. *Without Buddha I Could Not Be a Christian*. Oneworld, 2015.

Levine, Amy-Jill. *The Misunderstood Jew: The Church and the Scandal of the Jewish Jesus*. HarperOne, 2007.

Mackenzie, Don, Ted Falcon, and Jamal Rahman. *Getting to the Heart of Interfaith: The Eye-opening, Hope-filled Friendship of a Pastor, a Rabbi & an Imam*. SkyLight Paths Publishing, 2012.

Magida, Arthur J., and Stuart M. Matlins. *How to Be a Perfect Stranger: A Guide to Etiquette in Other People's Religious Ceremonies*. Jewish Lights Publishing, 1996.

Manseau, Peter. *One Nation, Under Gods: A New American History*. Back Bay Books, 2016.

McLaren, Brian D. *Why Did Jesus, Moses, the Buddha and Mohammed Cross the Road?: Christian Identity in a Multi-faith World*. Hodder & Stoughton, 2013.

Mosher, Lucinda. *Belonging*. Seabury Books, 2005.

———. *Loss*. Seabury Books, 2007.

———. *Praying*. Seabury Books, 2006.

Neusner, Jacob, Baruch A. Levine, Bruce Chilton, and Vincent J. Cornell. *Do Jews, Christians & Muslims Worship the Same God?* Abingdon Press, 2012.

Newell, J. Philip. *The Rebirthing of God: Christianity's Struggle for New Beginnings*. Skylight Paths, 2014.

Palmer, Martin. *The Jesus Sutras: Rediscovering the Lost Scrolls of Taoist Christianity*. Wellspring/Ballantine, 2001.

Patel, Eboo. *Acts of Faith: The Story of an American Muslim, in the Struggle for the Soul of a Generation*. Beacon, 2011.

———— . *Sacred Ground: Pluralism, Prejudice, and the Promise of America*. Beacon Press http://pluralism.org/, 2013.

Pavlovitz, John. *A Bigger Table: Building Messy, Authentic, and Hopeful Spiritual Community*. Westminster John Knox, 2017.

Peace, Jennifer Howe., Or N. Rose, and Gregory Mobley. *My Neighbor's Faith: Stories of Interreligious Encounter, Growth, and Transformation*. Orbis Books, 2014.

The Pluralism Project. http://pluralism.org.

Prothero, Stephen R. *God Is Not One: The Eight Rival Religions That Run the World—and Why Their Differences Matter*. HarperOne, 2011.

Rohr, Richard. *The Naked Now: Learning to See as the Mystics See*. Crossroads Publishing, 2009.

Sacks, Jonathan. *Not in God's Name: Confronting Religious Violence*. Schocken, 2017.

———— . *The Dignity of Difference: How to Avoid the Clash of Civilizations*. Rev. ed. Continuum, 2003.

Salkin, Jeffrey K. *Righteous Gentiles in the Hebrew Bible: Ancient Role Models for Sacred Relationships*. Jewish Lights Publishing, 2008.

Smith, Huston. *The World's Religions*. HarperOne, 2009.

Smith, Wilfred Cantwell. *The Meaning and End of Religion*. Fortress Press, 1996.

———— . *Patterns of Faith around the World*. Oneworld, 1998.

Thangaraj, M. Thomas. *Relating to People of Other Religions: What Every Christian Needs to Know*. Abingdon Press, 1997.

Volf, Miroslav. *Flourishing: Why We Need Religion in a Globalized World*. Yale, 2015.

Wertheimer, Linda K. *Faith Ed.: Teaching about Religion in an Age of Intolerance.* Beacon Press, 2015.

Wormald, Benjamin. "Religious Landscape Study." Pew Research Center's Religion & Public Life Project. May 11, 2015; http://www.pewforum.org/religious-landscape-study/.

Wuthnow, Robert. *America and the Challenges of Religious Diversity.* Princeton Univ. Press, 2011.